Praise for *Restless for More*

"Imagine what the world might look like if Christ's followers actually lived as He lived. Heidi McLaughlin gives us a glimpse, and then she offers practical strategies to show us how to do this. An excellent read, filled with real-life anecdotes and biblical teaching. Add this one to your library or use it for your small group studies."

—GRACE FOX, international speaker; author of *Moving from Fear to Freedom: A Woman's Guide to Peace in Every Situation*

"*Restless for More* gave me a glimpse into author Heidi McLaughlin's longing for others to experience the lavish love of God. Although her earliest memories of God were unpleasant, later on in her journey Heidi discovered the beauty and power of living in a relationship with God.

Read, and be prepared to catch her contagious passion for deeper intimacy with Almighty God found in places of being still and knowing 'that I am God.' You'll glean great practical ideas to make it happen, too. Thanks, Heidi, for this spiritually refreshing read. I loved it and pray that it reaches many restless souls!"

—RUTH COGHILL, author of *Woman of the Word (WOW series)*

"One of the greatest struggles in a woman's life is feeling restless. Heidi McLaughlin addresses this search for fulfillment in her latest book, *Restless for More*. Heidi's words will ring true with readers searching for more stability, more significance. She radiates Christ's greatest principle: When we love God and live out the "one anothers" from Scripture, our hearts are rooted in Him. We're no longer restless, because of His vine connection. We're filled full—the best fulfillment there is!"

—KATHY CARLTON WILLIS, women's speaker; author of *Grin with Joy*

"*Restless for More* is filled with heartwarming stories and insights into the lives of ordinary people who find blessing and great satisfaction serving God. Heidi draws the reader into finding fulfillment in unexpected places such as simple, and not-so-simple, acts of kindness and generosity. I love Heidi's honest delivery, and I am drawn to the beauty of who God continues to create her to be. This book will encourage readers to engage with the broken world around them and shine God's love."

—KELITA HAVERLAND, award-winning singer; songwriter, and speaker

"Heidi reaches into our most sacred hidden places—doubt, fear, and isolation—and ignites a beacon of light to expose the lies that trapped us there. *Restless for More* moves us to not only desire fulfillment in life but to expect it, through the power of Jesus Christ. If you long for more in life and desire a fresh biblical perspective to gain it . . . Be restless no more; this is a must-read for you."

—LINDA GOLDFARB, international speaker; author;
life coach and personality profiler

"In *Restless for More*, Heidi writes from a place of vulnerability, sharing her personal journey courageously while pointing you back to the source of her strength. Stories of family members and friends give even more depth to her message of accessible joy and unending grace. Heidi's gift for teaching and making biblical truth applicable will help you discover more about your gifts, your desires, and what you need to fulfill your soul."

—DR. SAUNDRA DALTON-SMITH, speaker; author of
Come Empty: Pour Out Life's Hurts and Receive God's Healing Love

"*Restless for More* leads readers on a great adventure to discover the incredible joy and fulfillment of refocusing on God's commands to love Him and serve others. With a simple and engaging style, Heidi McLaughlin weaves biblical truth with real-life stories to help you live out your purpose in truly fulfilling ways. Heidi shows you how to ignite a faith that allows you to live well and live free, using your abilities to serve others and develop relationships with eternal impact. This book is insightful, motivating, and challenging."

—JUDY RUSHFELDT, speaker; online magazine publisher; award-winning, multi-published author of *Making Your Dreams Your Destiny*

"*Restless for More* helps the reader find personalized, matter-of-fact solutions to their own nagging desire to walk closer to God. In a style that's unique, refreshing, and insightful, Heidi McLaughlin shares her proven methods, along with inspirational personal stories, such as how to leave a family legacy through a spoken blessing. A former widow, now remarried with a blended family, Heidi lives her life out loud and shouts hope for all step-families whose goal is family togetherness. This book is for any woman in any season of life, and especially valuable to those involved in counseling or mentoring. If you are in ministry, you would be would be wise to purchase extra copies of *Restless for More*. Keep one for your own use, to highlight and markup. Give others away to those who, like you, are anxious to be near to God and who deeply yearn to be like His Son."

—SHERYL D. GIESBRECHT-TURNER, ThD, founder and president of Transformed Through Truth, Inc.; speaker, radio personality, and life coach; author of *Experiencing God through His Names*

"In our world there is a heart epidemic of restlessness. Heidi isn't afraid to tackle the tough questions behind the unrest in searching for what it means to live fulfilled. It's the cry of the human spirit. With brilliant candor, she speaks to what we all might be thinking but are afraid to vocalize. *Restless for More* pulls back the curtain of the soul with authentic stories and life experiences that deliver the truth we desperately need to hear. With her gentle grace she encourages us to move toward what God desires—to be holistically content in Him. Heidi lives what she teaches and writes; she's wrestled with the hard stuff. You won't be disappointed. This book will trigger your longing to make more space for God and to live resolutely fulfilled."

—CYNTHIA CAVANAUGH, author of *Unlocked: Five Myths Holding Your Influence Captive*

"Heidi McLaughlin writes from her heart. Her passion and love for the Lord will challenge your heart and your actions. Sharing her own vulnerable stories, along with those of others, she provides realistic examples of how you too can be *Restless for More* 'one anothers' in your life."

—**JANET THOMPSON,** founder of Woman to Woman Mentoring; speaker, and author of many books, including *Forsaken God?: Remembering the Goodness of God Our Culture Has Forgotten*

RESTLESS
FOR
MORE

Fulfillment in
Unexpected Places

Heidi McLaughlin

In memory of my mother-
Hildegard Sawinski

Through your gentle, yet powerful example,
you taught your family to:

Be kind to one another,
Pray for one another,
And:
To love one another with a royal, lavish love.

CONTENTS

ACKNOWLEDGMENTS

FOR THE PAST FIVE YEARS I have lived out the stories and truths in this book. Through all of my challenges, pain, and joy, I have again discovered that nothing brings fulfillment and peace aside from God's command to love him and one another. I am profoundly grateful for the love and support of our delightful, funny, and kind, eclectic family. Their generous grace makes it easy for me to be creative, surrounded by cheerleaders who spur me on with: "Go for it, Mom, we know it will be great."

My darling Jack overwhelms me with patience and wisdom as he listens and gives insight into my endless questions and ideas. He covers me in prayer, helps me balance life and sleep, and allows me to unleash all the passion and purpose God has placed in me. I never knew I could love like this.

I am grateful for the friends who pray for me, especially my Skype prayer partners, Dr. Saundra Dalton-Smith and Sheryl Giesbrecht-Turner. Our common passion for speaking and writing connects our hearts in ways many people don't understand. Every month we share our praise items, burdens, and desires through an hour-and-a-half Skype prayer time. What peace to know that someone who "gets my heart" takes my prayer requests to our Heavenly Father.

Thank you to my publishers, Bill and Nancie Carmichael of Deep River Books, who stepped out with me in faith to let this book take flight. Thank you for believing in me.

My two beautiful partners, Grace Fox and Kelita Haverland, of our RADIANT Team who understand the dedication, hard work, and thrill of a speaking and writing ministry: It is such a gift to know I am not walking alone to help women grow into a deeper life with Christ.

What a gift to have the health and energy to take my regular five-kilometre walks to quiet my heart and hear the voice of my Heavenly Father. Those insights became the stories and words in this book. I acknowledge that the Holy Spirit guided my time, directed my research, and ignited my passion to help bring beautiful fulfillment to this world. I am a blessed woman.

INTRODUCTION

OUR FIRST DAYS navigating British Columbia's Okanagan Lake in a newly purchased boat thrilled us. Skimming over the water with sun on our cheeks and hair flying in the wind, we felt like we had just won the lottery. Then one day a wise friend said, "Once you've shown off the boat to all your friends and explored every inlet and park along the lake, the excitement will fade, and you'll want a bigger boat."

He's just jealous, I thought. *I can't imagine wanting anything better than this!*

Sure enough, restlessness crept in, and soon our boat felt too small, the motor not big enough and we craved something more impressive and shinier. Once we started looking around, we were amazed at the endless selection of beautiful boats, uniquely crafted to appeal to our every desire.

That's the job of the marketing companies. To show us what we don't have, so we feel a need. Then throw in the added belief that we deserve to have and do whatever makes us happy. Our restless spirits believe we will be happy once we have that next thing, and life will be better. So we work harder and buy more. Soon our plates are overloaded, but our souls are lonely and empty. Our restless nature is on a perpetual quest for the pleasure of a fulfilling life.

Let's start with a confession. We live in a consumer-driven, debt-loaded, and marketing-saturated world. We measure our worth by possessions, accomplishments, Twitter followers, number of "likes" on Instagram and Facebook, and our next exotic adventure or vacation. Somehow we got the idea we are entitled to do whatever it takes to make us happy. We have endless ways to pursue happiness. And we will stop at nothing to achieve it.

Fifty years ago, we measured success by our neighbour down the street, or the headlines in a newspaper or magazine. Today, global access bombards us with images of wealth, status, and success that evoke dissatisfaction in all areas of our life. *If they have it, why can't I? Surely I will be happy when I have a better husband, job, career, and more recognition.*

We lost our way. For over twenty years I have mentored and taught women to find their full potential in Christ. But, sadly, in the last three years I've heard too many women say something like this: "I am so stressed out I feel like I am going to have a nervous breakdown." I am deeply aware we are all trying to find happiness and meet the demands of life, but doing more doesn't fulfill us more. In fact, it robs us of our self worth and joy and makes us feel that whatever we do is never enough. These relentless and exhausting pursuits propel some people into disappointment, depression, eating disorders, addictions, and even suicides.

Our longing for fulfillment comes from the depth of our Spirit, and nothing in this material world will ever satisfy us for an extended period of time. Yes, we have those fleeting moments of undeniable pleasure, but often we wake up in the middle of the night, longing, and planning for "the next thing."

God has designed a glorious way for us to live. He wants us to experience fulfillment and joy through our relationship with him and one another. There is no other way. God gave us just one commandment, encompassing every aspect of our life: "Love the Lord your God with all your heart and with all your soul and with all your strength and with all your mind'; and, 'Love your neighbor as yourself'" (Luke 10:27 NIV).

This book will guide you to find satisfaction through the way God uniquely designed you. It starts by having an intimate, loving relationship with God, and then through applying the "one another" principles. I include true stories of people who applied these truths and found joy and satisfaction in their lives.

Each chapter ends with two life-changing applications.

FULFILL YOUR SOUL. Here I give you five or more steps—simple, practical ways you can fulfill your soul.

S.T.O.P. This is the place where you take your questions and allow the Holy Spirit, through the mind of Christ in you, to help you fulfill your life in ways you could never imagine.

S.T.O.P.
Stop and Ask God to Help You Fulfill Your Soul

BEGIN BY ASKING: Ask God a question.

S-Scripture verse. A verse will be available here for reflection.

T-Thanksgiving. Thank God for what he has the power to accomplish.

O-Observation. What would you like to ask God to do in your life?

P-Prayer. Ask him. I will end each chapter praying with you, because I am passionate about God fulfilling your life through the ways he designed you.

I may never have met you, but I've encountered women like you for the past twenty-five years. I have witnessed God's transforming power change people's struggles, converting the "never enough" emptiness into fulfillment and joy. I know he can because he is the King of kings and Lord of lords, creator of all life—including yours. It's time to take hold of what God has planned for you. It's time to be fulfilled.

I spent most of my life in pursuit of accomplishments and "stuff" to fill my soul. Always, I came up empty, feeling worthless, and wanting more. I wrote this book to guide you into the principles that will challenge you and make you ponder. But if applied, they'll take you on a pathway to fulfillment and joy.

CHAPTER 1

FULFILLMENT THROUGH GRACE

Refilling My Bucket

Seeing that a pilot steers the ship in which we sail, who will never allow us to perish even in the midst of shipwrecks, there is no reason why our minds should be overwhelmed with fear and overcome with weariness.
—JOHN CALVIN

WHENEVER I MEET WOMEN vulnerable enough to be honest about their feelings, all too often I hear this: "Heidi, I just want to be happy. But I'm so tired, frustrated, overwhelmed, and I feel empty. What can I do to find satisfaction in my life so I know I am finally enough?"

Too many of us equate our sense of self-worth with our accomplishments or net worth. I understand.

Restless, our souls long for that ultimate feeling of fulfillment.

At conferences, seminars, and workshops, I have heard it all. Speakers, leaders, and teachers, stand at their whiteboards drawing graphs and charts to show us that to find happiness, success, and fulfillment, there are things we can *do*. Simply de-clutter your life. Reschedule your priorities. Implement the next ten-step program to find balance and ultimate joy. I have been part of this teaching myself at times, so please don't burn me at the whiteboard when I say this: None of these steps bring lasting fulfillment. The focus is not to make life simpler, but rather to simplify and refocus our lives. The simplest, but often overlooked, road is to seek the one who will satisfy our lives so they overflow with joy. The Bible puts it this way: "Let your roots grow down into him and draw up nourishment from him. See that you go on growing in the Lord, and become strong and vigorous in the truth you were taught. Let your lives overflow with joy and thanksgiving for all he has done" (Colossians 2:7 TLB).

Whenever I mentor women or speak to an audience about finding joy and satisfaction, I ask them to visualize two buckets. I borrow this practical exercise from Bill Hybels' book *Simplify*[1], to help women discover why they feel so empty. I use two whiteboards. On one, I draw an empty bucket; on the other, a full bucket. Then I ask some questions.

THE FULL BUCKET

"How do you feel when your bucket is full?" I ask the audience. Then I go on to explain. Your bucket is full when you're getting enough sleep, your relationships are in good order, and you're eating properly, when you feel connected to God, when you have margin in your life, when you're on a good exercise program, and you're finding time to savor the moments. Your bucket is full when you feel so energized you want to shout, "Bring it on!"

Next I invite women to come up to the whiteboard and write down their responses. Without hesitation, they eagerly line up and start writing some of the following comments:

I feel joyful, content, and kinder, and I have more compassion.

I am able to make better decisions.

I don't get so frustrated.

I have more energy.

I sleep better.

I laugh easier.

I am less critical.

My words are sweeter.

I feel closer to God and I feel fulfilled.

THE EMPTY BUCKET

Then I ask, "How do you feel when your bucket is empty?" Your bucket is empty when you are sleep-deprived and overwhelmed, when you are always running from one activity to the next without any time for yourself, and when you are overworked and frustrated trying to meet everyone's demands. When there is nothing left for you. Your bucket is empty when you feel that despite everything you do, it's never enough.

The women now line up at the whiteboard and furiously scrawl some of the following words:

Angry
Depressed
Sad
Close to tears
Suicidal
Hopeless
Frustrated
Lonely
Resentful
Mean
Overwhelmed
Anxious
Like running away
Like giving up

Whenever I see these words on the empty bucket, my heart aches for all of us who try to fill our buckets by doing even more—bankrupting our souls. It's no wonder we keep trying harder; we are on a relentless quest to discover the right formula that will ultimately complete us.

We continue to feel restless because there is always more out there. Slick advertising constantly points out everything we are missing. By showing us what we don't have, TV commercials and even Facebook, Instagram, and billboards easily foster dissatisfaction and unhappiness in our lives. We are bombarded with the lie that we would all be slimmer if we eat Special K for breakfast, wealthier if we buy the right house insurance, prettier if we use the right shampoo, and more successful-looking if we drive a certain brand of car.

We continue to feel restless because there is always more.

The Bible tells us there is a rich life available to us, but there's one small problem. "The thief's purpose is to steal and kill and destroy. My purpose is to give them a rich and satisfying life" (John 10:10 NLT). The thief out there is named Satan. He wants to keep us away from an intimate relationship with God by derailing our thinking. Satan is on a quest too. To steal our joy and leave us feeling empty.

I am all too familiar with the empty bucket. I've felt unfulfilled, restless, and sad. The story of Elijah helps me to refocus and refill my bucket.

Like many of us, the Prophet Elijah had been very busy. In 1 Kings 18:21–40 we find that Elijah had a showdown with 450 prophets of Baal to show them who was the Lord. The Baal-worshipers built an altar, and so did Elijah. All day the Baal-worshipers called on their gods to send down fire to light the wood on the altar. By nighttime nothing had happened, and now it was Elijah's turn to put on a display proving whose God was real. After Elijah gallantly and confidently built the altar, he dug a three-foot trench, and poured four barrels of water over the altar until it overflowed into the trenches. Then he called on God to send fire to the altar. Suddenly fire flashed down from Heaven, burning up the altar, the stones, and the dust. It even evaporated all the water in the ditch (1 Kings 18:38). Then Elijah and his men grabbed the 450 prophets of Baal and killed them all. When Queen Jezebel heard what Elijah had done, she was furious and said, "You killed my prophets, and now I swear by the gods that I am going to kill you by this time tomorrow" (1 Kings 19:2 NLT).

Even after accomplishing great tasks for God's Kingdom, when Elijah heard Queen Jezebel was going to have him killed, he ran into the desert, sat under a broom tree, and prayed that he might die. His words were, "I've had enough. Take away my life. I've got to die sometime, and it might as well be now" (1 Kings 19:4).

Life is like that. Trying so hard to do everything right and please everyone. But our schedules are full, we feel trapped, and we don't know how to stop. Our buckets are so depleted we just want to disappear. It's never enough.

This story had a tremendous impact on my life because I have felt Elijah's discouragement. I've given everything I had and then felt unappreciated and lonely. It has helped me find a pathway to new hope and ways to refill my bucket. I love that the Bible is always so practical; always pointing us back toward rekindling and refocusing our attention to God. Let's look how this story can help us refill our buckets:

GET REST

Elijah lay down and slept under the broom tree (1 Kings 19:5). This is such a practical tip, it's often overlooked. Sleep is so important to us, and yet this is an area where we think we can steal some extra time. Sleep insufficiency may be caused by social factors such as round-the-clock access to technology and work schedules.[2] The bright lights on our iPads or the vibration or "ping" of our iPhones seem more important than getting the proper sleep we need. Sleep deprivation is now linked to increased motor-vehicle crashes and industrial disasters, and it can bring on chronic diseases such as diabetes, depression, obesity, as well as cancer.[3] My husband, Jack, and I have a saying: "Fatigue makes cowards out of us." Deprived of sleep, we speak unkindly to each other, become frustrated easily, and make poor decisions.

GET UP AND EAT

God is a Heavenly Father who is generous, kind, practical, and ready to meet us at every point of our need. He sent an angel to help Elijah regain his strength, and he gave him just what was needed next: bread and water (1 Kings 19:5–7). Elijah needed nourishment for his body before he could get up and replenish his soul. Seems too simple, doesn't it? But that's what you and I need as well. When we are busy, we don't take time to enjoy meals with our families around the kitchen table. We eat on the run, often without paying attention to nutrition. During busy times I do things I would never dream of doing—eating a quick meal from a drive-through and topping it off with a sugar-loaded soft drink. We need the right nourishment for the physical strength to tackle our empty buckets.

MEET WITH GOD

The angel helped Elijah regain his strength so that he could run to Mount Horeb to meet with God. Elijah looked for God in a windstorm, earthquake, and fire, but God was not in any of those powerful visual displays of power. Elijah found God in the sound of a gentle whisper (1 Kings 19:11–12).

In 2010, I came to this pivotal point in refilling my bucket. I'd spent too many hours walking up and down the corridors of our local hospital, looking after my ailing mother. In the same year, my son Donovan, an associate professor at the University of Las Vegas, Nevada, called and told us he was getting a divorce. If I had four good days in a row, I thought I was winning. I had to remind myself: despite what everything looks like, God is always working in the background.

Despite what everything looks like,
God is always working in the background.

At the hotel where I was to be the keynote speaker for a weekend event on the tough topic of Surviving Sabotage, a bright and inviting conference room greeted me, beautifully decorated in the unconventional colors of pink and orange. The ambiance of such striking colors put a smile on my face. This gave me an idea. When I returned to Kelowna it was time to plant spring flowers, and I used that stunning color combination in all the pots on my deck. Each morning as I watered my flowers, I lingered and smiled at the beauty of the contrasting brilliant colors. Those moments brought light and joy into my dark days. Eventually, I shared my pink-and-orange discovery on

Facebook and Twitter, and soon people were sending me pink and orange napkins, candles, cards, and luggage tags. Those gifts and colors delighted my spirit and added bright spots of hope to my empty days.

During that painful summer, I had many conversations with my son. One day he said, "Mom, in spite of all my efforts, it looks like I'm getting a divorce." I begged him to come home so that Jack and I could love on him by taking long walks and having deep conversations with him. After he arrived, Donovan and I chose a perfect September morning to walk through the magnificent vineyards on our side of the city.

We chose a route I had been walking for fourteen years, but for some reason that morning I was compelled to end it differently. In the middle of our rhythmic steps and intimate conversation, we saw something that startled us. Abruptly we stopped. Our jaws dropped as we stared at a banqueting table, placed in the middle of one of the rows in the vineyard. The table setting was majestic: fine china, cutlery, fruit, breadbaskets, wine glasses, and a napkin beside each plate. A stunning banqueting table, fit for royalty. And draped over the back of each chair—a linen shawl in the glorious colors of pink and orange. I was overcome with emotion at this display of beauty and splendor. It felt like an intimate nudge from my Heavenly Father, who wanted to give me a tangible reminder that he was aware of my pain, knew every detail of my life, and wanted to delight me. God's love washed over me as I remembered these words in the twenty-third Psalm: "You prepare a table before me in the presence of my enemies. You anoint my head with oil; my cup overflows."

God knew that my enemy at the present time was the fear of the unknown, sadness for my son's pain, the loss of my mother's health and independence. He knew about the myriad other small difficulties that robbed my peace and left me with an empty bucket.

When Donovan went back home to Las Vegas, I felt like I could breathe again. I gave myself permission to get excited about an upcoming trip during which my husband and I would speak at conferences in two different Polish cities and then move on to visit family in Germany.

I had not returned to my birthplace in Germany for over fifty years, and I yearned to revisit the days of my youth. But six days before we were to embark on our European trip, Jack looked at me tearfully and said, "My doctor told me they discovered a cancerous mass in my gall bladder, and we have to cancel our trip." The word for "broken" in Hebrew is *shabar*,[4] which is to "break in pieces, rend violently, crush, be shattered." That is how I felt as I sat with Jack in the colorless and somber hospital lounges. Endlessly waiting for more x-rays, exam results, the surgeon, and a surgery date. In 1994, my first husband, Dick, had died suddenly while playing basketball, and I was gripped with fear that I might become a widow once again.

But despite the upcoming challenges, I was determined to stay connected to God by deliberately making time to read the Bible and pray for healing and strength.

As I read throughout the New Testament I was amazed how many verses were about being thankful. Why had I never noticed these before?

Instead remind each other of God's goodness and be thankful.
Ephesians 5:4 NLT

And whatever you do or say, let it be as a representative
of the Lord Jesus, and come with him into the presence
of God and Father to give him your thanks.
Colossians 3:17 NLT

And always be thankful.
Colossians 3:15 NLT

Don't be weary in prayer; keep at it; watch for God's answers,
and remember to be thankful when they come.
Colossians 4:2 TLB

I heard my answer when I came across the next verse that told me it was God's will for me to be thankful. "Be joyful always, pray continually; give thanks in all circumstances; *for this is God's will for you in Christ Jesus"* (1 Thessalonians 5:18 NIV, italics mine). When the Bible tells me that something is "God's will for us," I need to pay attention because I know there is something in that command to help me live a better and satisfied life. So I began to study the word *thankful*, and I was amazed what I discovered.

The word thankful in Greek is *eucharisteō,*[5] which quite simply means, "to be grateful, thankful." Inside the word *eucharisteo* is the Greek word *charis,*[6] which means, "grace," or "that which affords joy, pleasure, delight, sweetness, charm, loveliness." So that means if I give thanks, I will find pleasure, sweetness, and other good qualities to help me refill my bucket and find new joy.

But there was more. The last discovery affirmed my assumption, and I was delighted with my new revelation. Tucked inside the root word of *eucharisteo* is also the Greek word *chara,* which means "the cause or occasion of joy."[7] This affirmed my discovery that if I give thanks, I will be reminded of God's grace, and joy will return.

I was overjoyed and excited about this new realization, but how would I put the thankful verses into practice? As I sat in more waiting rooms, I read through my beloved, favorite book of Ephesians. In Chapter 3, I was reminded that the Apostle Paul was imprisoned for Christ, in chains, and yet in verse 20, he was able to declare: "Now glory be to God who by his mighty power at work within us is able to do far more than we would ever dare to ask or even dream of—infinitely beyond our highest prayers, desires, thoughts or hopes."

I knew there were powerful truths to be learned from this verse. I was about to discover how it was part of God's plan to help me redirect my pain.

Now glory be to God: We need to give glory to God right in the middle of our chaotic circumstances, our pain, and our messes. Not tomorrow when we have the job, the adoption date, or the answers to our many questions. But right now, when we don't have any answers.

Who by his mighty power at work within us: We need to ask God to help us fill our buckets. To allow the Holy Spirit to give us the wisdom to know what really matters in our life, and to give us strength to let go of the things that don't have any value.

Is able to do far more than we would ever dare to ask or even dream of: When we seek God and ask for his help in our difficult circumstances, he wants to help us. We live in a per-formance-oriented society, and many of us feel that we can't count on anyone to help us. Everything seems to have a price tag or string attached to it. It can be hard to simply receive the love and adoration of our Father, who wants to do even more than we can imagine.

Bible commentaries refer to this verse as a doxology,[8] which is a liturgical expression of thanksgiving and praise to God. If Paul, in his dreadful circumstances, could be so thankful that he wanted to exalt and adore God, I also wanted to express my thanksgiving through a doxology. But how would I start? Then God gave me a picture in my mind of the pink and orange banqueting table in the vineyard. Out loud I exclaimed: "I knew you were there!"

Soon my hands flew over the keyboard. I don't know how long I sat there, but when I was done, my keyboard and t-shirt were wet from my tears. I had met with God, and I knew that while I was in his presence he spoke to me and poured his *charis-grace* on me. I had been soaking in the Father's love.

These were the raw and unedited words I wrote:

> *Yea, though I walk through your glorious vineyards,*
> *My soul is heavy and dark from disrupted plans and an unknown future.*
> *Yet you prepare an orange/pink banqueting table in the presence of my sadness.*
> *You feast my eyes with delight and fill me with surprise.*

Though the dark waves of doubt and lies hasten to engulf me,
You place treasures on my path to remind me
THAT:
You are the one and only true God—nothing is too hard for you.
You are omnipotent, yet intimate.
You are mysterious, yet full of promises.
You are invisible, yet reachable.
You are unpredictable, yet always faithful.
You are far, but always near.
You surprise me, but you are always able.
You point out my selfishness, then fill my cup.
You break me down, then build me up.
You give me desires, but nothing fulfills me like your love.
You say I am your delight, yet you are the one who brings me delight.
You woo me, love me, put up with me, listen to me, hurt me, and then transform me.
You are three-in-one, yet you are the only one.
You are the door to my future.
You are able.
Nothing is too hard for you.
I choose to trust you because you are God.

When I finished, I knew I would be all right. I'd met with God, and he'd reminded me that he was involved in every detail of my life. He assured me that nothing could separate me from his love, and that he was able to look after me in spite of my unknown circumstances. I did not know what Jack's and my future held, but I knew God would be right beside us, guiding us and helping us every step of the way. When I finished the doxology, my bucket was refilled with new hope, and gratitude spilling into joy.

Many of us can relate to Elijah when he collapsed underneath a broom tree in the middle of the desert. In the same way the angel helped Elijah to get his rest, eat nourishing food, and then meet with God, this example can also help us fill our own buckets. When we feel overwhelmed, exhausted, and alone, we often reach for anything that will make us feel better. I fully believe God allows these circumstances in our lives to learn to trust him more, and to use the wisdom we have gleaned to guide us into a more resilient and satisfying future. He never wastes our pain.

FULFILL YOUR SOUL

My pink and orange vineyard encounter, and knowing that God is involved in every detail of my life, has changed the way I live. How reassuring to know that God wants to put a smile on my face and delight me with something as unpredictable and unusual as a beautiful color combination. He wants all of us to learn to trust him, so he can help us fill our buckets with goodness that's fulfilling. "But to put their hope in God, who richly provides us with everything for our enjoyment" (1 Timothy 6:17 NIV).

Trying to fill all the empty spaces in our life—our closets, wallets, living rooms, purses, and garages—will eventually deplete our resources and our souls. In his book *Satisfied*, Jeff Manion states it so clearly: "I want for you to be freed from this treadmill. I so deeply want you to enjoy what you have without being deceived into thinking that it can fill something it was never designed to fill or fix something it was not intended to fix."[9]

Here are seven ways to keep your bucket filled by staying connected to God.

1. Imagine your heart as a bucket, and take inventory of what is going on in there. Your shopping expeditions, circle of friends, recreational activities, and how you spend your time and money, all determine what ends up in your bucket. "Guard your heart above all else, for it determines the course of your life" (Proverbs 4:23 NLT).

2. If your bucket feels empty, ask the Holy Spirit to show which items in your life are out of balance. Are your children overly involved with too many activities? Do you stay up too late at night

on social media? Do you work too many hours? Are you involved in too many recreational activities? "He is the Holy Spirit, the Spirit who leads into all truth. The world at large cannot receive him, for it isn't looking for him and doesn't recognize him. But you do, for he lives with you now and some day shall be in you" (John 14:17 TLB).

3. An empty bucket is a sign your plate's too full and your soul is left wanting. Are you spending time reading God's word, praying, and listening for his answers to direct your life? Make a deliberate choice to meet with him every day. He is the only one who can help you.

4. One of the best choices I ever made was to start a Gratitude Journal. One notebook is full and I am recording more items into another beautiful, new journal. When you stop to be thankful for what you already have, it helps you change the way you view your circumstances. It refills your bucket in an unusual and practical way. Consider starting your journal and see how it will change your life.

5. Getting the proper amount of rest seems too simple to make much difference in our lives. But it does. When we get the proper amount of sleep, we feel like a million bucks, ready to tackle the day with energy and passion. If you are going through a rough, sleep-deprived period in your life, go to a close friend or your doctor and ask for help. The lights from your phone and iPad screen stimulates your brain, keeping you awake, so turn off all screens by 9:00 or 10:00 at night.

6. Friends, family, and even your church may try to help you refill your bucket. But ultimately it is between you and the Holy Spirit, because this is a matter of the heart, not a nice, prescribed formula.

7. Try writing a doxology. Find a quiet spot, close all doors, quiet your heart, and listen to what God wants to tell you about himself. The words he will give you will impact you and remind you how much your Heavenly Father loves you and wants a deep intimate relationship with you.

S.T.O.P. AND ASK GOD TO HELP YOU
FULFILL YOUR SOUL

BEGIN BY ASKING: *God, what depletes my bucket?*

S-Scripture: "School's out; quit studying the subject and start *living* it! And let your living spill over into thanksgiving" (Colossians 2:7 MSG).

T-Thanksgiving: "Thank you, God, that your Holy Spirit will teach me how to start living a joyful life filled with thanksgiving."

O-Observation: Each day when my feet hit the floor, I want to start my life with purpose, joy, and hope, knowing that God is involved in every detail of my life. I know I have everything within me to experience this fulfillment, but I need the guidance and wisdom of the Holy Spirit to show me how to live out this reality every day. I want to know and experience the feeling of living with a filled bucket, overflowing with passion and energy to improve my life and make a difference in this world.

P-Prayer: "God, I want to know and experience what it means to have an intimate relationship with you. I desire to have the constant assurance you are involved in every detail of my life. I long to trust you and find hope beyond this present grind. Loosen my grip on meaningless stuff so that I can live with the joy and fulfillment that comes only from you. I lay my buckets before you and ask for your Holy Spirit to guide me into the truth of what needs to be added or removed from my life. Help me to be honest with myself, and to move forward with the courage to change the things I can. Thank you. Amen."

CHAPTER 2

FULFILLMENT THROUGH OUR ABILITIES

The Joy of Being Me

*Man cannot live without joy; therefore when he is
deprived of true spiritual joys it is necessary that
he become addicted to carnal pleasures.*
—THOMAS AQUINAS (1225–1274)

I HEARD SCREAMS as my body sailed across the cold tiles, my head barely missing the brochure display. People shouted, scrambling from all areas of the car dealership showroom with frantic questions: "Heidi, are you alright?" "Did you hit your head?" "Should we call an ambulance?" Gasping with pain and cringing with humiliation, I whimpered: "I don't have time to go the Emergency Ward. First thing in the morning I have to get on a plane to speak at a weekend conference."

Wincing with pain from my freshly sprained ankle, I hobbled into the washroom to inspect the disastrous results. *How could I face hundreds of women when I was in horrific pain and my battered face and black eye made me look like I'd been in a barroom fight?* Throughout my speaking ministry I experienced many obstacles and challenges. Through fevers, delayed flights, lost luggage, and stomach flu, God always triumphantly helped me get onto that platform to proclaim his love and reflect his glory. But this was different. Outwardly, I was a total wreck.

At 6:00 a.m. the next morning I was limping with pain as I retrieved my suitcases from the baggage claim area of the Calgary International airport. Next came the awkward scuffle to heave them into the trunk of my rental car. This was not my final destination. I still had a 270-kilometer trip to the conference center. After driving for an hour and struggling to stay awake, I found myself in the middle of a late, freakish winter snowstorm. Fighting against the backlash of snow whipping my windshield from the semi trucks, I became so distracted and weary I knew I had to stop. I pulled off to the side of the road and prayed. "God, I know you gave me this speaking engagement, but right now I feel helpless and afraid. I need your strength and safety to get me to where I need to be."

After that prayer I slept for half an hour. When I woke up, I felt strong enough to tackle the rest of the trip. Exhausted and confused, I finally arrived at the conference center just in time for the first session. But before I left my room to meet with all the eager women, I huddled in pain and prayed again. "God I cannot do this without you. In spite of the ugliness of my black eye, swollen ankle, and weariness, I need women to see the beauty of your love and glory."

As I hobbled onto the platform and engaged the audience with my opening comments, a strange connection transpired between the women and me. When they saw my raw, vulnerable, battered state, somehow they came face-to-face with their own insecurities and brokenness. With open hearts, they eagerly listened to my messages of how we can be transformed into all God designed us to be. All weekend, women asked me: "How do I use my gift and passion to serve God?" "Why do I feel so empty?" "How do I know what God wants to do with my life?" "Why do I feel so stuck and yet restless?"

I clearly recognized that through my own vulnerability and weakness, God was able to use me to reveal his love in a visual and powerful way. I am so grateful that God gave me the gift and ability to speak to women audiences and teach them biblical truths and remind them that there is nothing more beautiful than a woman who knows she is loved. Teaching and mentoring women gives me joy and fulfillment beyond anything I could ever have imagined. But, it's not always easy and it doesn't always look perfect or turn out the way I imagined it. I have come to realize that it's not just what I do with my gifts and abilities. When I use what God has given me and reflect the glory back to him, he makes my life even more beautiful and fulfilling.

I love the way John Ortberg describes it in his book *The Me I Want To Be:* "This world badly needs wise and flourishing human beings, and we are called to bring God's wisdom and glory to the world. The truth is, those who flourish always bring blessings to others—and they can do so in the most unexpected and humble circumstances."[10] We all know there is more to life than our daily humdrum existence. One reason we feel so restless is because we want to know and experience the joy of feeling passionate and fully alive. The fact is, every one of us is hardwired with gifts and abilities that have the potential to ignite passion within us and satisfy our deepest longings. So how do we discover them?

> *Our restless nature longs to know and experience the joy of feeling passionate and fully alive.*

FINDING OUR JOY
Discovering our Gifts.

When we discover and use the gifts and abilities God has given us, we experience greater fulfillment than anything else on earth. In fact, we lack nothing. The Bible says: "God has given each of us the ability to do certain things well" (Romans 12:6 NLT).

In his book *Hidden in Plain Sight* Mark Buchanan says it so well: "Everything you need for life and godliness you have already. In full. You actually don't need any *more*. Not one thing—not a cotter pin or flat washer, not a doohickey or a thingamajig: nothing's been withheld. Everything required for *zoë*—abundant and flourishing life—and *eusebeia*—a deep and real commitment to what matters most—is intact. The life you've always wanted is already here. Right now. Not next year."[11]

No wonder hundreds of books have been written about how to discover our natural talents and abilities. It is vital to our souls to find out what we're good at. We are unique and complex humans created by an amazing God who gives us these endless abilities that ignite our passion and fulfill our purpose. In her book *Pathway to Purpose*, Katie Brazelton states it like this: "What God's gift of passion will do for you, though, is set you free to live without guilt or uncertainty about what you should or should not do to please God. If you simply do what he designed you to do and be, you will find significance beyond measure."[12]

One of the most defeating statements I hear (too often) is "I don't really have any abilities. I'm not good at anything." But I beg to differ, because I know—and many studies show—that each human possesses from 500 to 700 different skills and abilities.[13] Unleash your natural abilities by asking yourself some simple questions:

- What do I love doing so much that I lose track of time when I am doing it?
- What keeps me awake at night and makes my heart pound with excitement when I think about doing it?
- What gifts and abilities have other people affirmed?
- Do I like working with people or by myself?
- Do I like creating beauty, solving complex problems, or organizing?
- What things have I done well?

Let your friends and people you trust help you shape these abilities. Listen to comments like:

- "You really pay attention to detail when you organize meetings."
- "Wow, you sure know how to set a beautiful table."
- "You write great introductions. Have you ever thought about becoming a writer?"
- "I see how you handled that child over there. Have you ever thought about opening a day care?"
- "You seem to care about women's issues. You would be great at mentoring another woman or facilitating a Bible study."

Those statements may be the key that opens the door to greater possibilities for you to enjoy whom God made you to be. Too often we try to fulfill the expectations of our parents, spouses, or even our friends, to be someone we are not. People may want you to be a lawyer or accountant, when in fact you love the freedom of your own hours in creating web designs or designing landscapes. When we are not using our best gifts, we dread going to work, we wake up with a sour attitude, we work harder, do more, achieve less. We feel drained and continue to be restless.

On the other hand, when we invest the best hours of the day in a job, opportunity, or commitment we are suited for, we have more energy, we feel confident, and we exude joy. God gives us these gifts to unleash passion and ultimately fill our longings in unique ways.

So let's carve out deliberate time to discover the abilities that bring us joy. The Bible says, "So since we find ourselves fashioned into all these excellently formed and marvelously functioning parts in Christ's body, let's just go ahead and be what we were made to be" (Romans 12:5 MSG).

Oftentimes we have difficulty determining our special abilities because they flow so easily and naturally. For example, I find incredible joy in preparing our home for company. I love to create beautiful bedrooms with fresh flowers, fluffy towels in the bathrooms, gifts baskets with water bottles, chocolates, and the latest magazines. It doesn't faze me one bit to have six people for dinner, or a group of thirty for an evening barbecue. I don't feel pressured or anxious; in fact, I love to see people enjoy every aspect of my preparations. Because I find so much joy and fulfillment in this activity, it's hard for me to understand other women's fear and reluctance to have people into their homes. Many find it so stressful. Several years ago, I did a gift analysis test and discovered that hospitality is one of my top gifts. I thought: *Really? That's a gift? How can that be when it comes so easy?*

I absolutely love to help people discover their natural talents. Learning to enjoy the abilities God has given me makes me long for others to find that same fulfillment and joy. For over thirty years, in a position of management, I directly supervised a number of women.

While performing interviews and annual reviews with my employees, I always reminded them that I was there to help them discover their natural strengths. I wanted them to succeed while still enjoying their jobs. When people find pleasure in what they are doing, they are the best version of who God created them to be.

Unleashing Your Gifts.

I stand in awe of the sheer mystery of the diverse abilities God has given to us. Out of billions of people, we all have different thumbprints, and no two of us have the same heartbeat. I love to see someone's face light up when they accept the fact that they are good with numbers or they can carry a tune. Or when they realize they are good at handling disruptive children, fixing a computer problem, or sewing costumes for a dance studio. Confidence rises up in that person and it makes them bold.

I saw my friend Joanne enter a fulfilling new phase of her life when she took a risk, making a bold choice to pursue the gifts and abilities God placed inside her. I was part of this journey of discovery when we were involved in Beth Moore's Bible study called *A Woman's Heart: God's Dwelling Place*, which explores the fascinating account of the building of the tabernacle. I explicitly remember the night we read how a Spirit-filled person was chosen to use their skills and abilities to build something beautiful for God. "God spoke to Moses: 'See what I've done; I've personally chosen Bezalel son of Uri, son of Hur of the tribe of Judah. I've filled him with the Spirit of God, giving him skill and know-how and expertise in every kind of craft to create designs and work in gold, silver, and bronze; to cut and set gemstones; to carve wood—he's an all-around craftsman'" (Exodus 31:1–5 MSG).

Oh the excitement when Joanne recognized that God could use her natural passion and beautiful gift of creativity to beautify our world, with the added bonus of fulfillment and joy. I was part of her life when she quit her job as supervisor in a bank to enroll in a two-year interior design program—later to start her own design company. I am sure I clapped the loudest at her graduation, seeing the display of her completed magnificent projects and plans for future designs. Over the next few years, Joanne was given the freedom to restore, redesign, and remodel our fifty-year-old church building. It was transformed into a glorious and beautiful facility. Joanne became the modern-day, Spirit-filled Bezalel, and I felt her joy. As she labored through tough chapters in her design course, her days didn't always go according to plan. Nor did they always align perfectly when she redesigned our huge old church. But she was fulfilled, because she was in her sweet spot. Her face exuded joy when design projects were completed and it gave her confidence to explore with paints, designs, and colors to hang her own unique paintings in her home.[14]

What a delight to witness firsthand how God can put a smile on our faces when we allow the Holy Spirit to give us courage to pursue the gifts God has placed inside us. It's not always easy, but there is no greater joy.

ENJOYING OUR JOY

As you read this chapter you might be wondering if you will ever discover those gifts that will bring you this fulfilling joy. At this point in your life, you may simply be surviving each day and trying to meet the demands of your job, family, and church. In her book *The Emotionally Healthy Woman,* Geri Scazzero asks great questions: "Am I being faithful to the life God gave me? How am I integrating my role as wife and mother with my own unique passions, talents, and limits so God's unique call on my life doesn't get swallowed up in the demands of ministry and family life?"[15]

For a period of my life, I functioned in survival mode. Each morning, I begged God to help me through the day. *Certainly there is more to life than just working hard each day and then falling into bed, exhausted and empty. I need to find things that bring me joy.* Over time, God awakened me to the fact that I am a very creative person, and I love beauty. Looking back, I realized that from the time I was twenty-seven, I was always looking for ways to explore my different passions:

- I took art classes at a college and eventually got lost in the sheer joy of exploring textures and colors of paints and creating pictures for friends and family.
- For years I sewed my own clothes and took sewing classes to help me create designer clothes.
- While living in the Canadian prairies for eleven years, I became fascinated with the different types of wheat and did "wheat weaving."
- I created fancy desserts, crocheted, landscaped, cross-stitched, decoupaged, and decorated homes.

In each stage of my exploration, all these God-given abilities gave me unique challenges but also absolute fulfillment. Eventually, there was a shift. I know that God gives us gifts and talents for pleasure and passion, but I realized I needed to expand my horizons. I prayed and asked God to help me find ways to bless others. From my late forties until today, God took my creativity and passions and morphed them into writing books and speaking at retreats and conferences. Looking back, it's easy to understand why my first book was called *Beauty Unleashed*.

It makes me smile to recognize that God zigzagged my steppingstones to prepare me for where I am today, speaking and spreading God's love throughout the nations. Nothing in our life is ever wasted. We are works-in-progress, in a state of being shaped into our most glorious existence. God designed us for a good life, which he perfects in us every day. Today is a good day for you to start pursuing and unleashing what God has placed inside you. The Bible says, "I am confident that the Creator, who has begun such a great work among you, will *not stop in mid-design but will* keep perfecting you until the day Jesus the Anointed, *our Liberating King, returns to redeem the world*" (Philippians 1:6 VOICE). In his book *Your Best Life Now*, Joel Osteen says it this way: "God wants you to have a good life, a life filled with love, joy, peace, and fulfillment. That doesn't mean it will always be easy, but it does mean that it will always be *good*."[16]

*Nothing in our life is ever wasted. We are
works-in-progress, in a state of being shaped
into our most glorious existence.*

REFLECTING OUR JOY

The Bible says, "Be delighted with the Lord. Then he will give you all your heart's desires" (Psalm 37:4 TLB). I love when we finally come to that place in our spiritual journey where we put God first, and he unleashes the kinds of desires we can pour onto a hurting and broken world. I hit my sweet spot and reveled in unbelievable fulfillment when I saw that my writing and speaking brought healing and joy to women audiences. But there was another, startling side to this journey that God needed to show me.

One day while I was in the midst of conference preparation, I felt God nudging me to open the Bible. I remember reading the verse over and over again, "I am the Lord! This is my name, and I will not give my glory to anyone else" (Isaiah 42:8 TLB). I was at the peak of my speaking career, and wherever I went I was enjoying favor from women and audiences. It was clear I was soaking up the applause and glory, as though my speaking ability was mine. It was a defining moment for me. Going forward I knew I had to acknowledge my writing and speaking abilities as a gift from God. I must always reflect that glory back to him. Our human nature is very greedy and needs a lot of attention and applause.

I am a work-in-progress, learning how to give the glory back to God. The book of John states it clearly. We Christians are, in fact, a reflection of his glory. "All who are mine belong to you, and you have given them to me, so they bring me glory" (John 17:10 NLT).

You and I are reflections of his glory. Once that reality hit me, it completely changed my speaking and writing. The following are some tips and steps I took to reflect the glory back to God.

- At the beginning of each teaching session, I have my audience stand up and acknowledge the ABCs of God's character. Then I tell the women that I am the messenger but God is the author of our life stories. "We do this by keeping our eyes on Jesus, the champion who initiates and perfects our faith" (Hebrews 12:2 NLT).
- I prepare my teaching sessions the best I can, not putting the focus on me but always trying to infuse my messages with God's love for my audience.
- I have stopped waiting for the applause or "thank you." I will often show a video to end the session and then walk off the stage.
- Whether my presentations are well received or they turn out messy (like my story at the beginning of this chapter), I believe God can use them for his glory in a way I might never understand.
- It's not about how good I am, but about being available for God to use what good I can do.
- God's gifts to me are, in turn, a gift to the world.

There is incredible freedom and ultimate joy when we allow God to unleash his gifts in us and when we in turn use those gifts to make a difference in other people's lives. Hopefully, this will make our world a better place to live. It may not always look the way we want it to, but we must believe they will be used for the ultimate good.

FULFILL YOUR SOUL

From my own experience I believe God uses our gifts and abilities in different seasons for different reasons. "And we confidently and joyfully look forward to actually becoming all that God has had in mind for us to be" (Romans 5:2 TLB). To fulfill your soul at this point in your life, consider how you can use your abilities in the stage you are in right now.

Enjoy who you are.

Don't look at someone else's accomplishments and wish you could be like them. They may already have experienced years of preparation or hardships to get them where they are today. Also, don't forget that while something might look good on the outside, we don't know what it's like behind closed doors. "Make a careful exploration of who you are and the work you have been given, and then sink yourself into that. Don't be impressed with yourself. Don't compare yourself with others. Each of you must take responsibility for doing the creative best you can with your own life" (Galatians 6:4 MSG).

1. If you have known your passions and gifts from the time you were a little girl or boy, consider yourself fortunate. For many people, including me, it takes a lifetime of exploration and discovery to find that sweet spot in your life. Start today.
2. Don't forget, your most obvious and powerful gift may be right in front of you. You may not recognize it because it flows so easily. Ask yourself, "How can I use this talent to glorify God and make a difference in this world?"
3. Take time to delight in God and spend time with him, reading the Bible and praying. The more your heart and desires line up with God's desires, the more he will use your abilities to make this world a little more glorious.
4. Don't undermine your gifts and abilities. It may be as simple as:

   • If you are a young mom, the way you read a book to your children.
   • If you are on a great career path, the way you help people around you to grow and flourish.
   • If you are an empty nester, this may be the time to mentor younger women or teach a Bible study.
   • If you love flowers, use them to bring a smile to someone's face.
   • If you love baking, cooking, or organizing your kitchen, use these skills to teach your children or a young mom.

5. Ask a family member or friend, "What do you think I'm good at?"

We have to be careful not to get discouraged when things don't work out the way we expected. Even though I know God has called me to write and speak, I encounter challenges and roadblocks as I live out this calling. Yet I know that each obstacle is there to help me depend more on God and learn to be faithful with what he has designed for me to do.

S.T.O.P. AND ASK GOD TO HELP YOU
FULFILL YOUR SOUL

BEGIN BY ASKING: *What gifts and abilities do I have that will make a difference in this world?*

S-SCRIPTURE: "In his grace, God has given us different gifts for doing certain things well" (Romans 12:6 NLT).

T-THANKSGIVING: "Thank you, God, for always pouring grace into my life. Thank you for making my gifts available to me, to learn to do well and enjoy."

O-OBSERVATION: I can hardly fathom that God has given me so many gifts and abilities to use and enjoy. I know that when I apply them the way God intended, I will find unsurpassed enjoyment and fulfillment. There is so much ugliness and pain in this world, so how can I use my gifts to bring beauty and reveal God's glory?

P-PRAYER: "God, I truly want to make a beautiful difference in this world. I desire to embrace all the gifts you have placed in me, but I need you to show me what they are. I must confess, some days it feels like the whole world knows what they are doing except for me. Often I feel so overworked and tired, I don't think there is any room in my life to explore the abilities you have given me, let alone to turn around and pour them out. Yet I believe that, ultimately, these gifts you have placed in my soul will bring me the most fulfillment I will find in this life. I place myself in your hands and ask you to gently guide me to discover my gifts and then to use them to bring glory to your name. Thank you. Amen."

CHAPTER 3

FULFILLMENT THROUGH LAVISH LOVE

A Royal Love Affair

*Our love to God is measured by our everyday fellowship
with others and the love it displays.*
—ANDREW MURRAY

I AM INFATUATED WITH my grandchildren. I feel fully alive when I spend time with them as they pull me into a world of singing silly songs, drawing outrageous dinosaurs, and making colorful Lego creations. The older grandchildren stimulate me with different delights. As I write this chapter, my husband, Jack, and I have just returned from Vancouver Island, British Columbia, where our grandson Ryan had the privilege to sing and dance in the role of Riff in the American musical, *West Side Story*. Surges of pride and pleasure flowed through my veins as I watched his musical talent and agility on the dance floor. He was spectacular.

During the rest of our time on Vancouver Island, we experienced a different joy. Over cups of steaming espresso we debated politics, golfing, and other controversial media news with our grandson Alex. Alex's keen mind absorbs fascinating data and gives us hours of honest and animated conversation mixed with bouts of laughter. Once we've reached our morning quota of coffee and debate, we head over to the golf course where we challenge each other's scores, grumble over lost balls, and high-five the occasional birdie and par.

I feel endless pleasure and fulfillment in these situations as my husband and I invest in our grandchildren's lives. It is important for me to know what gives them joy, makes them squeal with laughter, or what makes them sad and cry. I love to encourage them to use the natural talents, gifts, and creativity God has given them. Even though they all live in different parts of Canada and the United States, Jack and I make every effort to travel and spend time with them in their homes, or to have them come and spend time with us. Our home was designed and built with enough bedrooms and bathrooms so there would always be enough room for everyone to come and visit.

Over the years, we've marked my grandchildren's physical growth in pencil by height and year on the door molding outside the main bedroom. I get weepy when I see this tangible evidence of their growth spurts, which for some of them started as they received their nightly bath in the kitchen sink. Being intimately involved in their lives is the catalyst that keeps us in a loving relationship and continues to give me joy beyond anything I could ever have imagined.

God designed us to feel and experience joy. Rick Warren, in his bestselling book *The Purpose Driven Life* states, "One of the greatest gifts God has given you is the ability to enjoy pleasure. He wired you with five senses and emotions so you can experience it. He wants you to enjoy life, not just endure it. The reason you are able to enjoy pleasure is that God made you in his image."[17]

It's easy for me to find joy through my relationship with my grand-children. However, for years I could not fathom having that kind of intimate and pleasurable relationship with God. Over time, I discovered that finding fulfilling joy is not about money, stuff, or rules. It is simply about remaining close and connected with key people in our lives. This kind of sustainable joy is available to all of us, when we take deliberate steps to maintain intimate, loving relationships.

Over time I discovered that finding fulfilling joy is not about money, stuff, or rules.

To have a joyful relationship with God, we need to learn how to make ourselves at home in his love. The Bible puts it this way: "I've loved you the way my Father has loved me. Make yourselves at home in my love. If you keep my commands, you'll remain intimately at home in my love. That's what I've done—kept my Father's commands and made myself at home in his love. I've told you these things for a purpose: that my joy might be your joy, and your joy wholly mature" (John 15:9–15 MSG). What does it mean to be "at home" in God's love? Throughout the last twenty years I have finally learned how to find pleasure living in God's love on a daily basis. Three startling phases unleashed this discovery.

PHASE ONE: APPEASE

My earliest memories of God are very unpleasant. Our family's church was legalistic and governed by endless rules. "This is good and that is bad. This is right and that is wrong." Everything was categorized as black and white and there was no middle ground for grace. Through eight-year-old ears, I heard long and boring sermons about a God who was going to punish me and send me to hell if I did something "bad." I sat and looked at people's sour faces, surmising that there was no fun or joy knowing God. But still, I wanted to be a good girl and please my parents and God by being obedient to the endless demands of acting the right way and doing the right thing. When I was eleven, I made a deliberate decision to follow God. It wasn't through a joyful choice and a meaningful prayer; it was by deciding to follow a calendar. Every morning when I got up I made a rule that I would be a good girl today. If, at the end of the day, I'd succeeded, I gave myself a check mark on my calendar. At the end of two weeks, I was disgusted with my constant failure and the difficult and meaningless process. I gave up.

I was a creative child, full of life and always looking for ways to laugh and have fun. When I heard the new and exciting songs of the Beatle era and saw their stylish haircuts and cool clothes, all I wanted to do was get up and dance to the music. But, of course, dancing was another thing on the endless list of forbidden pleasures. I saw no value in all those restrictions, and I was tired of attending a church where there was no grace and joy. At seventeen, I was shunned and labeled as "worldly." I finally told my parents, "I have decided I don't want to go to church anymore." It just about broke their hearts, but I was true to my word and did not attend church again until I was thirty-two.

Looking back, I understand how the church and its leaders were trying to protect us from a destructive way of life by enforcing a list of rules. After all, God's moral instructions are for our good. But living to appease God by following man-made rules to avoid calamity is a potent mix for rebellion or pride. Most of us are insecure humans who want to control our own choices and destiny. When we feel we have someone watching our every move, ready to strike when we mess up, we get our backs up and say, "Nobody is going to tell me what to do!"

Rebellion.

Rebellion is an open resistance to rules and authority. I rebelled because I needed to break away from the ball and chain stopping me from pursuing my self-centered goals. It seemed like everyone around me was fixated on my behaviour, and everything was focused on external and visible actions. Did you wear the right clothes? Did you go to the movies? Did I see you smoking? Do you have a television in your home? Do you play cards on Sunday? In the Old Testament people continually rebelled and turned away from God by worshipping idols.

Now I recognize that our rebellion separates us from a God who is trying to protect and bless us. We set ourselves up for a possible pathway to self-destruction. "For rebellion is as bad as the sin of witchcraft, and stubbornness is as bad as worshiping idols" (1 Samuel 15:23 NIV). Looking back, I see that my rebellion was my own idol of saying, "I don't need anyone to tell me what to do; I can have joy and success my way."

Sadly, my rebellion separated me from God and set me on a path where I made many wrong choices. This caused my family and me many years of unnecessary heartache.

Pride.

Pride can have two meanings. One is an egotistic, over-inflated opinion of our own accomplishments and success. The other is a sense of satisfaction from having made good choices and actions. Inflated pride separates us from God by hardening our hearts and building a wall around us that says, "I am better than you, smarter than you, and I have all the right answers." Pride is an idol in our life that says, "I don't need anyone but me, because I have it all figured out." Jesus condemned this prideful behaviour, and he warned the pious, self-righteous leaders of the day. "Woe to you, Pharisees, and you religious leaders! You are like beautiful mausoleums—full of dead men's bones, and of foulness and corruption. You try to look like saintly men, but underneath those pious robes of yours are hearts besmirched with every sort of hypocrisy and sin" (Matthew 23:25, 26 NLT).

Because of my pride, I looked like I had it all together on the outside, while in reality my heart was empty, lonely, and searching for something to make me feel loveable and valuable.

Both rebellion and pride separated me from God. I could not understand that Jesus already knew everything about me, including my creative abilities and my need for laughter and joy. I couldn't fathom that he would accept me with all my faults and failures. In his book *With*, Skye Jethani says this about Jesus: "Jesus welcomed everyone, including those deemed unrighteous, to be with him. He was regularly seen in the homes of people believed to be on God's 'naughty list,' and he often shared his table with prostitutes and thieves . . . While the religious leaders sought obedience and conformity of behaviour, Jesus sought to welcome people back into relationship with God. He inspired love and compassion, not simply sacrifice."[18]

It took me years to discover I was good enough for Jesus to accept me, and he wanted me to make my home with him.

PHASE TWO: PLEASE

In 1978, I finally prayed and asked Jesus to forgive me for my sins so I could begin a personal and intimate relationship with him. But surprisingly, instead of becoming confident and enjoying my new freedom, I became a raging perfectionist. Because I had been bad for so long, I felt I needed to earn and prove my worth as God's adopted daughter. Don't misunderstand me; I knew Jesus died on the cross for my sins and I would be with God for all eternity, but I could not comprehend the concept of grace. I felt like I needed to make up for my years of rebellion and now I wanted to represent God well. For years, I wore myself out trying to show the world that Christians are perfect. I could not understand that I didn't have to repay God or earn my rightful place, as worthy of his love.

My outward actions and appearance would have convinced anyone I was a passionate and dedicated follower of Jesus Christ. My mouth never uttered a single word of profanity. I stopped smoking and set my internal monitor to be perfect in everything I did. Daily, I measured my value by what I achieved for God. I taught Bible studies, became a leader in my church, mentored women, and sang in the choir. The highest praise came from a woman who worked closely with me in a law firm: "Heidi, how can you be so perfect in everything you do?" Hearing those words, I felt I had at last achieved my rightful place as one of God's children. Except I did not know I had it all wrong, and my motives were completely skewed. I didn't understand the difference between perfectionism and being "perfect in him."

Perfectionism.

Perfectionism is a slippery, toxic slope of trying to be our own god. It is a fear-based desire to control our circumstances and the people around us, and to prove to the world that we are good enough. It indicates a self-absorbed, controlled plan to produce a perfect report card. We lay awake at night, measuring ourselves against some random standard of perfection, to see if we nailed it or missed the mark. It can leave us frustrated, anxious, and angry, or most often feeling that once again we are simply not enough. Anything less than perfection is failure, and every successful accomplishment is filled with pride. Perfectionism works hard to earn the right to be admired and loved.

I learned that I could never work hard enough or achieve enough success to earn God's love. It was hard for me to accept that God's love is a free gift to be received and enjoyed. "For it's by God's grace that you have been saved. You receive it through faith. It was not our plan or our effort. It is God's gift, pure and simple. You didn't earn it, not one of us did, so don't go around bragging that you must have done something amazing" (Ephesians 2:8–9 VOICE).

One day I looked in the mirror, and from the furrows in my brow I knew I was exhausted. Despite all the good things I was trying to accomplish, I still felt frustrated, anxious, and angry. I realized I had not yet released control of my own high expectations and accepted God's free and lavish love. I began to recognize the truth: "Yes, I am the Vine; you are the branches. Whoever lives in me and I in him shall produce a large crop of fruit. For apart from me you can't do a thing" (John 15:5 NLT). One day I said, "I quit trying to be perfect, it's just too hard," and took my first step of faith on a spiritual journey toward learning that I can do nothing apart from Christ. I began to let go of the tendency to control all facets of my life and to trust God to bring me fulfillment and joy.

Perfect in him.

Now I am grateful for that day when I hit the wall with exhaustion and said out loud, "I quit! I'm tired of trying to win everyone's approval or meet everyone's expectations including my own." That was the day I let go of the control of trying to orchestrate my own life and allowed the Holy Spirit to begin to transform my thinking from earning God's love to living in his love. Becoming "perfect in him" meant I was on a pathway to let Jesus live his life through me. It involved giving him all my failures, wrong motives, constant striving, and self-imposed messes and allowing him to bind up my broken heart and fill all my empty longings. This is a maturing process that would make me whole and healthy, but it will take the rest of my life. "Don't be mistaken; in and of ourselves we know we have little to offer, but any competence or value we have comes from God" (2 Corinthians 3:5 VOICE).

Through my deepest struggles and striving God reminded me I needed to make my home in him so he could assure me he would never leave or forsake me. He wanted me to find comfort and healing by soaking in his lavish love.

PHASE THREE: A ROYAL LOVE AFFAIR

It is important for me to connect with loved ones in my home. I believe our homes are the places where love needs to be experienced and shared. For years, I struggled with the story of Jesus visiting the home of Mary and Martha as told in Luke 10:38–41. I always saw myself as Martha busy in the kitchen, preparing food, arranging the seating, setting the table, and making sure everyone had a cool glass of water. I love the idea of Jesus coming into their home, a familiar place of friendship, hospitality, and nourishment. But I struggle with wishing I could have been sitting at the feet of Jesus like Mary did.

But someone has to attend to the food.

I believe our homes are the places where love needs to be experienced and shared.

My sweet mother taught me much about the balance between being a Martha and a Mary. My mother's home was always filled with the tantalizing aroma of a roast or chicken in the oven or apple streusel or German *beinenstich*[19] cooling on the counter. I learned much of my hospitality expertise from watching my gracious mother moving around in the kitchen and serving her family with love. But what my mother really excelled at was loving God and allowing his love to infiltrate every part of her life and soul.

After my father passed away in January of 1996 from ALS, better known as Lou Gehrig's disease, my mother gave us visible evidence of what it meant to soak in God's love. Her home became a place to unite family members, share meals, stories, and prayers. She made it very clear she didn't need more money, clothes, or new furniture to make her happy. My mother trusted that God "will supply all your needs from his riches in glory because of what Christ Jesus has done for us" (Philippians 4:19 NLT). Whenever I asked her if she was lonely she always replied, "No, I have God who is with me in my home every minute of the day."

A few years before mom passed away on November 26, 2013, she was experiencing dizzy spells. It was time for my younger sister Brigitte and me to take more deliberate steps to care for her. The nights when it was my turn to sleep at her home I knew I had to be quiet at 8:30 p.m. while my mother had her usual private time with God by reading the Bible and praying. While preparing my bed on the couch in the living room, I heard the familiar rhythmic sound of her voice talking to God. She prayed for each of her children and grandchildren by name. She praised God and thanked him for supplying all her needs. She thanked him for his lavish love, which gave her strength and hope for every moment of the day. She committed all her fears, thoughts, and praise to the one who she knew held her life in his hands. She had a love affair with her Heavenly Father, the creator of Heaven and Earth. My mother knew she was a child of the King of kings and the Lord of lords, and she was ready to be with him in Glory.

Weeks before mother died, my grandson Alex and my children, Michelle and Donovan, came to visit with her, to spend time holding her hand and loving on her. We all loved mother so much that we bustled around attending to all of her wishes. During her wakeful moments, she looked at us with great love in her eyes. Her words overflowed with thankfulness for all we were doing for her. With a smile on her face, she quietly said, "This is like a royal love affair."

So my life is not defined by whether I am a Mary or a Martha, because at times, depending on the needs and circumstances, I can be one or the other. But the most important part in whatever I am doing, whether engaged in hospitality or sitting in solitude with Jesus, is to focus on experiencing lavish love. Because when I asked my mother for the best advice on how to live this life, her words were simple. "Just love God and each other; that is the best thing you can do."

FULFILL YOUR SOUL

Our homes are places where we can learn and experience the highest calling of love. They are places where we can put down our iPhones, iPads, and other distractions to look into each other's eyes and share laughter and feel ultimate pleasure. It doesn't take any money or success to tell children silly stories at bedtime, play a board game, or throw bocce balls in the backyard. My grandchildren are happy with honest and authentic conversations and a bowl of their favourite ice cream. Walking the dog in California, jumping on the trampoline, or watching someone sink a birdie putt gives us stories and pleasures that fill our hearts to overflowing.

I am besotted with love for my whole family, but I know that God is even more in love with you and me. "This is how we know what love is: Jesus Christ laid down his life for us" (1 John 3:16). Learning to lean into and experience the lavish love of God will bring us more pleasure beyond anything we can buy or accomplish. Our homes can be places where we put love into action. Here are six ways you can do that:

1. Stop trying to appease or please and just learn to accept and experience your Father's love. Is there something you are still doing to earn your Father's love? Isn't it time to let it go?

2. We love to experience freedom, intimacy, and authenticity of being ourselves when we spend time with the people we love. When I spend time with God in his beautiful creation I feel close to him and I can be honest about every difficulty I am going through. I find great joy and fulfillment when I talk to God about the different trees and flowers, and delight in the beautiful landscape colors of the four seasons. The next time you go for a walk, tell God you delight in his Creation, and imagine how that will put a smile on his face.

3. When I learned to accept myself the way God designed me, I became less afraid of rejection. This opened my heart for God's love to flow into my spirit. It was as though I opened the door of my

heart to him and I began "to feel at home with him." When we accept each other's flaws, irritations, and differences, we will begin the wonderful journey of learning to lavishly love on each other.

4. It is important you set aside all distractions including your technological devices, so you can engage in honest and crucial conversations. Necessary words, soaked in love, help you dismantle misunderstanding and awkward barriers.

5. Making your home with God is not much different than preparing a loving home for your family. It takes intentional time, regular efforts for good discussions, intent listening, and an unwavering desire to build strong and lavish love relationships.

6. Parents and mature members of the family need to model what it means to learn to trust God by talking to him in prayer. Our children need to see us bowing our heads and thanking God for our meals. They also need to see us hold hands and release our worries and anxieties to the one who holds the answers in his hands.

S.T.O.P. AND ASK GOD TO HELP YOU
FULFILL YOUR SOUL

BEGIN BY ASKING: *How can I learn to live at home in your love?*

S-Scripture: "I have loved you even as the Father has loved me. Live within my love" (John 15: 9 NLT).

T-Thanksgiving: "Thank you, God, that you accept and love me just the way I am and I don't have to earn your love."

O-Observation: God wants me to receive his lavish love. I love that this Bible passage uses the terminology of "living in God's love." To me this implies a home where people learn to love each other through intimate and loving relationships. I learn to love God by spending time with him, talking, listening, and trusting him enough to let him orchestrate my life. When we live together in homes, we also get to know each other's character. I need to spend more time reading the Bible, so I can get to know God's loving and faithful character.

P-Prayer: "God, in this moment I want to live in your love by simply stopping and basking in your loving presence. While I am on this mysterious journey of learning how to "live at home in your love," I open my heart and give you permission to cast away all my previous notions of what love is, and embrace everything you want to teach me. I also open my home and soul to love others, for that is a sign that your love is beginning to make its home in me. Thank you for your lavish love. Amen."

CHAPTER 4

FULFILLMENT THROUGH SOLITUDE

My Red Suitcase

We live, in fact, in a world starved for solitude, silence, and private: and therefore starved for meditation and true friendship.
—C.S. LEWIS

DREAMS DO COME TRUE, *thank you God. I can't believe I get to speak at a women's conference in Lexington, Kentucky on the uplifting topic of "Refreshing Our Hearts with Jesus."* I was still pinching myself as I Googled travel options. It would be a long and exhausting trip, but what does that matter when I am fulfilling the desires of my heart?

The alarm clock jarred me into reality just in time to get to the Kelowna airport and check in my two large suitcases. Thirteen hours later, I landed in the Lexington airport exactly as planned. The trip was unfolding without a hitch, until I arrived at Baggage Claim. With delight I spotted the green, animal-print suitcase that held my books, but the one I really needed was the nice, shiny, red one. Without the red suitcase I would be in real trouble as it held all my clothes and essentials for four speaking sessions. I finally realized I was the last woman standing in the baggage department and I had to accept that my red suitcase didn't make it.

After a grueling drill at the baggage-claims counter, I was given a website address to track the progress of my lost luggage. The stern attendant reassured me there were planes flying in from Chicago all the time, and that my missing suitcase would be there first thing in the morning. "Don't worry," she said. "It will all be fine."

The next morning I woke up at 6:00 a.m. with a fever and a raging stomach flu. I realized I was very sick when I barely had the energy to call down to the reception desk and ask about my lost suitcase. "No, Mrs. McLaughlin, your suitcase has not arrived, but don't worry—planes fly in from Chicago all day long."

Fortunately, my first speaking session was not until 7:00 that evening. When I am fortunate enough to have a bonus day all to myself, I catch up on CNN news, my reading, check my e-mails, or write my next blog. That day I intentionally decided to put my personal work aside and seek God. I needed him to prepare my heart for my speaking sessions, and to ask him for help in recovering my red suitcase. All morning I lay flat on my back, reading my Bible, talking to God, asking him for healing for my stomach flu, and praising him for this opportunity to be in Lexington. I am a visual person, and God speaks to me through pictures. At 11:30 a.m., I was startled when God gave me a picture of a luggage tag.

After a puzzling examination of my tags and matching them up with the numbers listed on the website, I realized the airline was searching the wrong luggage. After an agonizing hour, talking to various people in different countries, I managed to convince the airline to change the tag numbers on the website and restart the search by looking for the right suitcase. With this mission accomplished, I lay back on the bed, exhausted. For the next four hours, I prayed, praised God, and then listened. At 4:00 p.m., I was still sick and did not have my much-needed red suitcase. At 4:15 p.m. I prayed: "God, would you please *show me* where my red suitcase is."

Within minutes, God gave me a mental picture as clear as a snapshot. It was the picture of my red suitcase standing behind the United Airlines counter, underneath the United Airlines sign. I have learned to trust God with my pictures, so immediately I called the Lexington airport. After many voice messages, I finally connected with a young and pleasant airport security employee. I wish I could have seen his face when I asked him, "Would you be good enough to take a minute and walk down to the United Airlines counter. Underneath the sign you will find a red suitcase." After a long, awkward pause, he replied, "Yes, ma'am, I'll do that for you." Two minutes later, this kind young man came back and told me, "Yes ma'am, there is a red suitcase sitting under the United Airlines counter." With a smile on my face, I asked him if I could have a taxi come and pick it up, and he replied, "No, ma'am, I will deliver this suitcase to you. Where do you live?"

When this young man walked into the hotel with my red suitcase, I hugged him and said, "Thank you for your kindness. Did you know that today you are one of God's angels?" He smiled and said, "Ma'am, you're more than welcome."

I had my red suitcase, and even though I was still sick, in faith I prepared myself for my first speaking session. Once I walked onto the platform, all my flu symptoms disappeared, and I knew I was in the presence of Almighty God who turns our disappointments into miracles. His loving nature wants us to cry out to him to help us in our time of need. He wants to speak to us, if we will only listen. "For the eyes of the Lord search back and forth across the whole earth, looking for people whose hearts are perfect toward him, so that he can show his great power in helping them" (2 Chronicles 16:9 NLT).

My weekend in Kentucky renewed the knowledge that when I give my restless nature and frustrations to God and take the time to seek him, he will take my doubts and disappointments and turn them into greater faith and fresh joy. Treasures more beautiful than I could ever imagine. Only God can provide answers, healing, and fulfillment in my soul that can't be achieved in any other way.

HIDDEN POWER

When I think of how my life has taken shape over the last thirty-five years of my spiritual journey, I see how the things I longed for most did not happen the way I envisioned. Often my perfectly implemented plans were disrupted or changed, and I was left feeling disappointed or thinking I was a failure. Yet over these precious years, God continues to surprise me with the greatest treasures birthed out of the most tragic and disappointing circumstances. When I unclench my fists, release my perfectly formed plans, and seek his wisdom and presence, God continues to delight and fulfill me beyond my wildest expectations. Over time I have learned that God just wants my whole heart, my full attention, and my daily agenda. The way to find this incredible power is in places of silence and solitude. The Bible tells me: "Be still and know that I am God" (Psalm 46:10 NIV).

The way to find God's power is in places of silence and solitude.

The Hebrew word for "know" in this verse is *yada*: "to know by experience, to recognize, admit, acknowledge, confess."[20] This indicates taking the time to get to know someone intimately. It's not about gathering more information or living up to a certain standard. Also, it's not about more meaningless conversation, like yadda, yadda, yadda. To know someone deeply, we need to pull away from our distractions, relinquish our agendas, and open all parts of us that are true and false. We must create a space away from all the noise and over-stimulation, where we can become vulnerable and give God our deepest desires, greatest disappointments, pain, and longings.

The distractions that prevent us from knowing God intimately come from many sources. For example the ping of our cell phones and the swoosh sound of another e-mail coming into our inbox seem to take precedence over almost every activity. Even though technology was supposed to help us and make our lives easier, its intrusion fragments our relationships and sabotages our moments of solitude with God. In her book *Sacred Rhythms,* Ruth Haley Barton states, "I am noticing that the more I fill my life with the convenience of technology, the emptier I become in the places of my deepest longing. I long for the beauty and substance of being in the presence of those I love, even though it is less convenient. I long for spacious, thoughtful conversation even though it is less efficient. I long to be connected with my authentic self, even though it means being inaccessible to others at times. I long to be the one who waits and listens deeply for the still, small voice of God, even if it means I must unplug from technology in order to become quiet enough to hear."[21]

I completely agree with this author, but I will go one step further. When I speak at conferences, I use the phrase "solitude is power." I have many reasons and examples to back up this radical statement.

RADICAL POWER

I live in West Kelowna, a city separated from the main part of Kelowna by the huge Okanagan Lake. Consequently, in order for us to drive to downtown Kelowna, we have to cross a bridge. In 2005, construction started on the new three-lane bridge, which was to replace the older and largest floating bridge in Canada.

Every day as I drove to work over that rickety old bridge (built in 1958) I eagerly looked for signs of progress on the new bridge. For the first two years, I saw nothing. Soon construction started on the bridge deck. Throughout the next year as the bridge took shape, all I saw was a majestic concrete giant. Eventually it looked like a bridge. Then, it officially opened in 2008 as the William R. Bennett Bridge. It's such a masterpiece, it was showcased on the Discovery Channel on October 28, 2009.

Over the three years that I waited for the new bridge to take shape and open up, I became fascinated with the building process. I became acutely aware that the greatest amount of work and most strategic parts of the bridge happened below the waterline. That is where the foundation was built to form and uphold the road portion of the bridge. Such support needed to be strong enough for the 50,000 cars that would cross each day.

It affirmed that my soul power and fulfillment for every area of my life comes from the places no one else sees. I need to build the unseen part of me, my inner spiritual core, to be so strong and resilient that it will carry me through the burdens and challenges of each day. Now I know that this beckoning in my soul for solitude is a call from God so he can build a strong foundation in my life through his radical power.

*My soul power and fulfillment for every area of my life
comes from the places no one else sees.*

TRANSFORMING POWER

Solitude is defined as a state of isolation or seclusion. It is a state of being alone without being lonely. That is hard for us, because we are always striving to be a good neighbor, a successful employee, a good Christian, or a good son or daughter. But it is in solitude we can look deep into our souls and contemplate the question Jesus asked the blind beggar, Bartimaeus, in Mark 10:46–52.

This story took place in the city of Jericho, which, even though it is surrounded by desert, is a popular holiday resort thanks to its freshwater springs. That is the city Jesus was passing through on his way to Jerusalem when the blind beggar Bartimaeus shouted, "Jesus, Son of David, have mercy on me!" People around him tried to shush him. "Be quiet!" some people yelled at him. Everyone knew that beggars were social outcasts. Why would Jesus want to have anything to do with them? So Bartimaeus ignored the shouts of the throngs and pleaded even louder. "Son of David, have mercy on me!" He got right to the point without excuses, whining, or explaining of status. He needed Jesus, and he didn't care about his disadvantaged position as a blind beggar. When Jesus heard this cry for help, he stopped and said to the people around him, "Tell him to come here!"

Next is one of the most soul-searing and kindest questions Bartimaeus would ever hear. Jesus asked, "What do you want me to do for you?"

"Teacher," the blind man said, "I want to see!"

Don't most of us just want to stop being so blind about the falsehood of the world that we can see the truth that will help us find ultimate fulfillment? Jesus wants us to pull away from the crowds, shush the naysayers, turn off our cell phones, and experience more of him. "And when you draw close to God, God will draw close to you" (James 4:8 NLT).

Solitude is a choice. It is not about being lonely, but about making an intentional decision to be alone with God and allow him to transform our soul. Going to church, attending Bible studies, and being involved in a small group at your church are all wonderful and fulfilling exercises. But I agree with Dallas Willard in his book *The Great Omission*. In a chapter where he states that we need to attend to our own spiritual formation, Willard says: "We have counted on preaching, teaching, and knowledge or information to form faith in the hearer and counted on faith to form the inner life and outward behavior of the Christian. But, for whatever reason, this strategy has not turned out well. The result is that we have multitudes of professing Christians who well may be ready to die but obviously are not ready to live, and can hardly get along with themselves, much less others."[22]

Here are eight examples of how solitude unleashes God's power and transforms and fulfills our lives.

1. **We give Jesus our deepest desires**. Let's start with the question Jesus asked the blind beggar. "What do you want Jesus to do for you?" When we become honest and vulnerable and give Jesus the deepest desires of our hearts, we open ourselves to give him an opportunity to speak to us. Over time, we see how he orchestrates our lives to bring us the opportunities and life changes we are looking for.

2. **We learn to recognize God's voice**. When the prophet Elijah waited to hear God's voice, he did not hear it in the fire, earthquake, shaking of rocks, or violent wind. In a still, small voice, Elijah heard God say to him, "Why are you here, Elijah? *What is it that you desire?*" (1 Kings 19:13 VOICE). We can't hear God when we allow external noises to demand our attention. We have to learn the different ways God speaks to us. God speaks to me through images, the beauty of his creation, and his Word. Pay attention to how God speaks to you. God wants to communicate with us, but it takes time and silence.

3. **We learn to listen so we can find our abundant life.** "Come to me with your ears wide open. Listen, and you will find life" (Isaiah 55:3 NLT). Many people don't think God speaks to them. But he wants

to communicate with us through many different ways, so he can fulfill our lives. When I heard God nudge me to look at my luggage tags, I listened, and it changed the course of my entire weekend. It gave me incredible joy, but it also gave me new hope and reassured me he would be with me in my future struggles.

4. **God recalibrates our reality and gives fresh hope**. Whenever I read the news, I feel numb, sad, and sometimes angry. Is it possible to find joy and fulfillment when there are theatre shootings, political disagreements, family break-ups, and constant chaos? Yes, some days the external world can crush us. But, just like my story of building the Kelowna Bridge, the parts we don't see, or the internal parts of our life, strengthen and anchor us. We build on our internal strength when we use our solitude to read the Bible and learn more about God's promises and faithful character. Even though it looks like our world is out of control, God has the ultimate plan, and he can be trusted with every aspect of our life. In *The Great Omission,* Dallas Willard says, "Knowing Christ through times spent away in solitude and silence will let our 'joy be complete' (John 16:24). It will bring over us a pervasive sense of well-being, no matter what is happening around us."[23]

5. **Solitude allows the Holy Spirit to teach us truths**. The Bible says: "But you have received the Holy Spirit and he lives within you, in your hearts, so that you don't need anyone to teach you what is right. For he teaches you all things, and he is the Truth, and no liar; and so, just as he has said, you must live in Christ, never to depart from him" (1 John 2:27 NLT). Over the past thirty-five years, I've had moments in my career when huge problems led to more questions and no answers. Sometimes I had documents in front of me that were so confusing I was sure there was no way out. When I took those problems and questions to God and asked him for an answer, and when I took the time to listen, he gave me answers in the most marvelous but unusual ways. They came through an e-mail, a conversation, a magazine, writing on a billboard, or a blog.

6. **In solitude, our hearts are unburdened.** "Give your burdens to the Lord. He will carry them" (Psalm 55:22 NLT). Throughout the Psalms, King David laid himself bare before God and told him just how he felt. When you and I are honest with God, we can feel free to let our words flow without condemnation.

> I am forgotten like a dead man, like a broken and discarded pot.
> Psalm 31:12 NLT

> You alone can lift my head, now bowed in shame.
> Psalm 3:3 NLT

> I plead with you to help me, Lord, for you are my Rock of safety.
> If you refuse to answer me, I might as well give up and die.
> Psalm 28:1 NLT

> Oh Lord, I try to walk a straight and narrow path
> of doing what is right; therefore in mercy save me.
> Psalm 26:11 NLT

7. **Through inhaling and exhaling, we find spiritual miracles.** When we stop and inhale the beauty of God's Spirit, his glorious creation, his lavish love and kindness, and then exhale our resentment, offenses, insufficiency, and troubles, our hearts will make room for the peace of God to find its way into our soul. Linda Evans Shepherd, in her book *Experiencing God's Presence,* puts it this way: "A spiritual miracle is a miracle of emotional or spiritual well-being or healing, and the good news is that this kind of miracle is always God's will for us. A spiritual miracle can include things such as getting right with God, being healed of bitterness, or experiencing the relief of God's forgiveness of sin."[24] Inhale God's unfailing love; exhale anxiety and angst.

8. **Solitude restores our joy.** Love is our deepest longing and it brings us the greatest fulfillment. David G. Benner put it this way in his book, *Surrender to Love*: "God's love is the source and

fulfillment of all creation. From the beginning, God's love has been evoking life in all its abundance. It is 'the passion, the oxygen, the flame, the glue-fueling, firing connecting the universe in its amazing array.' Apart from the ever-creative outflow of God's love, there would be nothing but darkness, void and nonbeing."[25] When we are reminded of this glorious expression of someone who loves us, joy returns and overflows.

Had I not taken the entire day in Kentucky to seek God, I know without a shadow of a doubt my red suitcase and I would never have been reunited. When God finally gave me the picture of my suitcase, I was as excited as a little kid in a candy shop. Taking deliberate time to seek God in solitude, and leaning in to listen, is like learning to live.

FULFILL YOUR SOUL

I believe there is a restless spirit within all of us. You are reading this book because you want to experience more of God's power in every area of your life and in every season. One great way to start is by finding that quiet place where you surrender yourself to God's love and discover all he wants to do in your life. Here are five ways to fulfill your soul.

1. Find your rhythm. Prepare a special chair and comfortable place in your home to meet with God every day. Find a rhythm that works uniquely for you. An article in *Today's Christian Woman* explains it as a withdrawing from our addictions. "Silence is the time when we withdraw from our addiction to noise, words, and activity. And so in silence we withdraw from our own inner compulsions, not just the expectations of other people, but from our addiction to our own thoughts and words."[26] We develop this rhythm of silence and word. For example, some people love to read the Bible cover to cover and journal; others like to read certain favorite chapters and simply meditate on them. Explore your rhythm until you fall in love with the fact that you have an appointment with God each day. It is God who wants to make you prosperous and successful. "Study this Book of Instruction

continually. Meditate on it day and night so you will be sure to obey everything written in it. Only then will you prosper and succeed in all you do" (Joshua 1:8 NLT).

2. Do a "Walk and S.T.O.P." Some years ago, I did this with several friends and found it fun and fulfilling. Here is how it unfolded:
   - We met in a park with our Bible and notebook.
   - We walked, talked, laughed, and soaked in God's marvelous landscape.
   - Next, each of us found a private spot under a tree or close to the water.
   - We were given a certain chapter in the Bible and instructed to read it two or three times.
   - Then we did the S.T.O.P. version of journaling in the same way it's done at the end of each chapter in this book.
   - After twenty-five minutes, we came back into a circle and shared what God taught us during our time of silence and solitude.
   - *Awesome.*

3. Listen to quiet praise music and worship. Your best rhythm might be found worshiping and praising God while you listen to your favorite worship music. Take time to light some candles, turn off the lights, and soak in the presence of God through meaningful worship music. "I will sing to the Lord as long as I live. I will praise God to my last breath! May he be pleased by all these thoughts about him, for he is the source of all my joy" (Psalm 104:33–35 NLT).

4. Open your hands. Take time to sit quietly and open your hands, palms up, to God. Imagine giving him all your anxiety, questions, resentment, and disappointment. Take time to be vulnerable and give yourself permission to cry. Picture God taking the broken pieces of your life and replacing them with a gold heart. "Let him have all your worries and cares, for he is always thinking about you and watching everything that concerns you" (1 Peter 5:7 NLT).

5. Because God is love, and we are made in his image, the point of our existence is to learn to love. During your solitude time, read all of 1 John and 2 John. Then, throughout the day, find practical

ways to practice love. The Bible commands us to do this: "My dear children, let's not talk about love; let's practice real love. This is the only way we'll know we're living, truly living in God's reality" (1 John 3:18, 19 MSG). Rick Warren talks about God's passionate love for us in his book *The Purpose Driven Life*. "Why did he bother to go to all the trouble of creating a universe for us? Because he is a God of love. This kind of love is difficult to fathom, but it's fundamentally reliable. You were created as a special object of God's love! God made you so he could love you. This is a truth to build your life on."[27]

We all need to build our life from the inside out. That is our place for strength, beauty, and power.

S.T.O.P. AND ASK GOD TO HELP YOU
FULFILL YOUR SOUL

BEGIN BY ASKING: *God, what part of my spiritual foundation do you want to build?*

S-Scripture: "May you experience the love of Christ, though it is so great you will never fully understand it. Then you will be filled with the fullness of life and power that comes from God" (Ephesians 3:19 NLT).

T-Thanksgiving: "Thank you, God, that you want me to know and experience your extravagant, generous, and endless love. Thank you that despite my weakness and imperfections, you dispense love into my spirit so lavishly and freely. Thank you that you can take my restlessness and striving and replace it with the fullness of life."

O-Observation: Despite all my hard work and striving, I still feel empty and tired. I recognize that I need to pull away from all expectations and distractions and go into a place of silence where I can be honest with myself and bare my soul before God. I am beginning to understand that even though this world is wonderful and has much to offer, all the material stuff will never satiate the secret longings of my heart.

P-Prayer: "Heavenly Father, just as you heard the cry for help and mercy from the blind beggar Bartimaeus, I know you also hear my cries for help. Have mercy on me and help me to be honest with those things in my life that make me restless and deplete my soul. I look to you to fulfill the desires of my heart by helping me build a strong foundation from the inside out. I give you my hopes, dreams, and daily plans, and I ask you to transform them into your will for my life. Ignite my spirit to seek a place of beauty and quiet where I can read the Bible and get to know you. I ask that you pour your love into those empty, gnawing places in my soul and help me to know what real fulfillment feels like. Thank you for helping me. Amen."

CHAPTER 5

FULFILLMENT THROUGH LOVING CONNECTIONS

One Is a Lonely Number

Cherish your human connections:
your relationships with friends and family.
—JOSEPH BRODSKY

I COULDN'T PUT IT OFF any longer. I needed the courage to venture into our walk-in closet to change from my church clothes into something more casual and comfortable. My husband, Dick, had died three days prior, and thus far I had been unable to face the horror of seeing his clothes in the closet hanging next to mine.

I stood and marveled at Dick's shirts, always lined up so perfectly. Except for one sleeve. It must have been the last shirt he wore before he went out to play basketball. In his hurry, he hadn't hung it up quite properly. My eyes stayed glued to that one blue sleeve. *This must be the last shirt he wore and didn't have time to put away properly. He will never come back to wear this shirt. He will never again wear any of these shirts or walk into this closet.*

My forced and stoic composure that I had faked at church that morning crumbled, and I fell to the floor on my knees. Dick's death finally hit me. He would never come back. I was alone.

Sobbing uncontrollably and with fury, I pounded the closet room floor. My body shook and tears streamed down my face. I screamed at God, "Why did you let this happen? I've spent years honoring you and serving you. You said you would never leave me or forsake me. Where are you now? When I really need you, I feel like you have completely abandoned me."

In the middle of my explosive anger, I experienced unusual warmth. It felt like warm oil flowing from my head, down into my arms, through my whole body, then down to the tip of my toes. My anger and shaking stopped. Peace flowed through me as though I had been held and hugged. It could only be the Holy Spirit, the Comforter that Jesus said he would send. "I will ask the Father to send you another Helper, the Spirit of truth, who will remain constantly with you" (John 14:16 VOICE). The Comforter, our *parakletos* [28] who is summoned, called to one's side, especially called to one's aid.

Without a shadow of a doubt, I knew God's Spirit was with me in that room. He knew my excruciating pain and was there to comfort and give me new strength. He was faithful to his promise. "Never will I leave you; never will I forsake you" (Hebrews 13:5 NIV). I will never forget that holy encounter, experiencing his lavish love.

The days, weeks, and months ahead were dark, and my grief was beyond any pain I had ever experienced, but I knew that God had not abandoned me on this lonely pathway.

DESIGNED FOR CONNECTION

We crave connections. We want to know we are loved, valued, and that there is a special place of belonging. It's important to know that someone delights in us, someone with whom we can share our failures and successes, and who will call forth the goodness in our hearts. Whether this is in a marriage relationship or friendship, God knows we need to be connected first to him, and then to one another. The Bible says, "And the Lord God said, 'It isn't good for man to be alone; I will make a companion for him'" (Genesis 2:18 TLB). You and I are created in the image of God, who is a Trinity: God, Jesus, and the Holy Spirit. That is the complete picture of a divine, intimate, and perfect connection. Our souls are designed for a fulfillment only heaven can provide. But while we are in our human body, we need one another to bring us into the experience of sharing God's work within us.

Larry Crab states it well in his book *Connecting*: "The power is found in connection, that profound meeting when the truest part of one soul meets the emptiest recesses in another and finds something there, when life passes from one to the other. When that happens, the giver is left more full than before and the receiver less terrified, eventually eager, to experience even deeper, more mutual connection."[29]

---

*Our souls are designed for a fulfillment
only heaven can provide.*

Even though we may not be aware of our inner quest, our restless nature is always seeking this ultimate connection. Our restlessness started in the Garden of Eden, where God invited Adam and Eve to dine lavishly in an abundant garden. They were to enjoy every tree except one. Except one! Therein lay the temptation to want what we can't have. In his book *Satisfied,* Jeff Manion explains what happens this way: "Do not gaze upon what he has given. Fix your eyes instead upon what he has withheld. Now, desire . . . deeply desire that. God isn't really good. He is holding out on you. Do not focus on what you have but instead upon what you lack."[30]

And so, our first parents, Adam and Eve, went after the one thing they were not allowed to have and stumbled into sin, which separated mankind from God. We continue to look around and see what we don't have. Our emptiness makes us think we are missing out, and we ache for something more. That gnawing can be so bad that it becomes a problem demanding a solution. We don't recognize our ache as a need for connection with God and each other, so we do whatever it takes to relieve it.

People who try to live a fulfilled life on their own strength can succeed for a certain time, but eventually they will start to feel detached, abandoned, isolated, and then alone. Neither money, nor success, nor all the material luxuries will satisfy their deepest longings. If they can't share their victories, sorrows, and accomplishments, they will feel deeply alone. Disconnected.

DISCONNECTIONS

The restlessness and longing in our souls is like an empty space or vacuum. As far back as circa 485 BC, the physicist-philosopher Parmenides said, "Nature abhors a vacuum."[31] A vacuum cannot exist, because it goes against the laws of nature and physics. This also applies when there is a void in our spiritual soul. If we do not fill it with God's love and intimate connections with each other, we will find ways to consummate the beckoning of our desires.

Social Media.

In our present culture, social media is causing a serious dilemma of loneliness and depression. We look at other people's lives and walk away with the feeling that "I am only as good as the number of 'likes' I get on Facebook or Instagram."[32] People who spend much of their time in a virtual world become isolated and lonely. In their book *The Digital Invasion,* Dr. Archibald D. Hart and Dr. Sylvia Hart Frejd give us some great insight: "It is not surprising, therefore, that we have seen an increase in the incidence of isolation and loneliness in the young at a time when social media is on the rise. Too many people lock themselves into 'virtual living,' rather than interact with others in real-life circumstances."[33]

Not only do we begin to feel lonely, but we also become depressed. The authors go on to say, "Studies now show that too much time spent on Facebook and other social networks can cause 'Facebook Depression.' It is a form of depression that is created by comparing yourself too much with others on Facebook. Keeping up Facebook facades and making comparisons as we have described can breed a deep sense of discontentment. These distortions can ultimately trigger a deep depression because you can't live up to the false standards that social medical mostly presents."[34] Because we only feel as good about ourselves as the pictures we see and the words we think, we feel like a nobody. Not enough. Weak. Insignificant. But here is the good news. We don't need to look for our significance on Facebook. God's word says it clearly: "That means we will not compare ourselves with each other as if one of us were better and another worse. We have far more interesting things to do with our lives. Each of us is an original" (Galatians 5:26 MSG). The first step to removing ourselves from excessive social media is recognizing the dangers.

Pornography and computer games.

When I searched for statistics on this topic on Google, I was overwhelmed with 2,960,000 results. So I turned to the trusted book written by my friend Dr. Sylvia Hart Frejd, *The Digital Invasion*. The facts are so complex and disturbing, I will only give you highlights:

> *Gaming.* "Gaming provides a make-believe world for the gamer, providing an escape from the real world. Some play for many hours each day, disregard personal hygiene, and become so involved with their gaming interactions that they ignore their broader lives. It disrupts their sleep patterns and they focus entirely on their game achievements rather than on other life events."[35]
>
> *Pornography.* "Internet pornography is number one in all categories of Internet sales. It is accessed more frequently than games, travel, jokes, health, weather, and jobs combined. The average age of the first exposure to Internet pornography is now eleven years, and some studies say it is as early as eight and a half years of age"[36] "The excessive use of video games and online porn in pursuit of the next exciting thing is creating a generation of risk-averse guys who are unable (and unwilling) to navigate the complexities and risk inherent to real-life relationships, school, and employment."[37]

God did not create us for isolation, which harms our bodies and souls, but for meaningful connection, which has the power to squelch our restless pursuit and give us joy. The first step to overcoming this emptiness is to get honest with our feelings and recognize our deep need for pleasure and intimacy. Online encounters create an illusion of a more exciting life and greater pleasure, but in the long run they leave a person bereft and only wanting more and more. This can lead to relationships breaking down, emotional disorders, irritability, a secret, double life, and even suicide.

Overspending.

When the going gets tough, it's time for retail therapy. Compulsive shopping is a felt need to fill an inner void, perhaps from childhood depravation or a need to gain control. Shopping is also a way to distract from a difficult reality and to express power by pulling out a credit card and showing the world you are a "somebody."

But how often do we hear, "I'm so deep in debt, I don't know how I will get out"? Or, "I don't know if I will be able to make this month's mortgage payment"? And it's not just about retail therapy. Our present society is obsessed with working longer hours, earning higher wages, and having more. We have the impression money will buy us happiness. This causes much pain in relationships, business associations, and even in whole countries. In his book *Simplify,* author and pastor Bill Hybels says this: "Grown men and women have buckled over and burst out crying as they told me their stories, because of the self-hatred and shame associated with mishandling their finances. I've too often seen the long-term effects in people's lives when they live as slaves to money. Guilt and shame leave an indelible mark."[38]

It is a wonderful thing to have money when it is used in productive and healthy ways to provide for our families and make a difference in this world. Money is not the problem. It's the lure of its power, thinking it will solve all our problems, fill a void, and provide us with endless joy. When we overspend to quiet the restless longings of our soul, it puts us in bondage to lenders. Eventually, this all comes crashing down and leaves us bereft, suffocating under the heavy burden of guilt and shame. The Bible says it this way: "For the love of money is at the root of all kinds of evil. And some people, craving money, have wandered from the faith and pierced themselves with many sorrows" (1 Timothy 6:10 NLT).

Busyness.

One of our most deceptive and distorted ideas of how to fulfill our restless souls is thinking we need to do more. In the last two years, I've had several women tell me they are so busy they feel like they are going to have a nervous breakdown. Most of us would never commit a crime such as murder, theft, or adultery, and Satan knows he can't deceive us with these big, obvious sins. But as long as we're moving fast, Satan can keep us distanced from connecting with God and each other—the intimate and ultimate source of our joy and fulfillment.

Often we use busyness to show people how important we are, but do we even realize that these attempts at fulfillment are in fact depleting our souls? Our busyness puts up walls of self-sufficiency and pride, and drowns out God's special purpose for our lives. In the parable of the soils, the Bible puts it this way: "The thorny ground represents the heart of people who listen to the Good News and receive it, but all too quickly the attractions of this world and the delights of wealth, and the search for success and lure of nice things come in and crowd out God's message from their hearts, so that no crop is produced" (Mark 4:18, 19 TLB). How sad it is, that this subtle deception is causing extra work, fatigue, and emptiness.

One of our most deceptive and distorted ideas of how to fulfill our restless souls is thinking we need to do more.

Shame.

When we feel flawed, we feel shame, so we run and hide. We have been doing this since Adam and Eve disobeyed God in the Garden of Eden: "I heard you in the garden, and I was afraid because I was naked: so I hid" (Genesis 3:10 NIV). Shame is deeply rooted in us when we feel we do not measure up. Believing we are too imperfect or damaged to be worthy of acceptance in society, we pull back and hide behind our jobs, busyness, arrogance, and pretense. We check out mentally and emotionally, and become estranged to the world.

We feel shame when we are not smart enough.

Not right enough.

Not athletic or thin enough.

Not confident enough.

Not good enough Christians.

Not pretty enough.

Not in the right neighborhood.

When our credit card is declined, when we scream at our children, when we miss an appointment, run out of gas, lose our job, or say something stupid. The list is endless, because we are all imperfect people.

Shame is like wearing dirty underwear. For people who've worn it for a long time, it becomes a familiar part of their existence. It becomes their identity. They think they are hiding their shame from the world, but the ugly truth is that they are the ones in captivity. They can't fight it, because it is intangible. But here is how to move on.

In her book *Daring Greatly,* Brené Brown puts it this way: "Own your story. Don't bury it and let it fester or define me. I often say this aloud: *'If you own this story you get to write the ending.'* When we bury the story we forever stay the subject to the story. If we own the story we get to narrate the ending."[39] Shame thrives on secrets that are kept in the dark. The greatest power in releasing shame is to become desperate and vulnerable enough to tell your stories to a counselor, spouse, or trusted friend. To help us become brave and resilient, we need to pray and ask Jesus to help us. "Those who look to him for help will be radiant with joy" (Psalm 34: NLT). I know from personal experience that God will answer your prayer. He'll give you the courage to tell your story, and you will be amazed and shocked by how freeing it is. Healing will follow.

ONE IS A LONELY NUMBER

All of the above disconnections are barriers and false illusions of what we think will feed our restless souls. One day, we will stand face to face with God, in our resurrection bodies, fully alive, and beautifully complete. In the meantime, we are stuck in these mortal, earthly bodies, and we continue to struggle to feel whole. Yes, we will experience those perfect moments in time when we catch glimpses of heavenly perfection. But while we are in the process of being transformed from glory to glory, our greatest fulfillment will come through our connections with our Creator and one another.

Through our disconnection, we become isolated and lonely. Mother Teresa said these heart-wrenching words: "The greatest disease in the West today is not TB or leprosy; it is being unwanted, unloved, and uncared for. We can cure physical diseases with medicine, but the only cure for loneliness, despair, and hopelessness is love. There are many in the world that are dying for a piece of bread but there are many more dying for a little love. The poverty in the West is a different kind of poverty—it is not only a poverty of loneliness but also of spirituality. There's a hunger for love, as there is a hunger for God."[40]

Loneliness has become a universal problem. It is a dreadful feeling, like pain, nausea, emptiness, and darkness in the pit of your stomach. We feel this when we are isolated or when we think that no one understands or cares. People are lonely sitting behind their computers, in Senior Assistance homes, in their workplaces, and even within their families and churches.

After my husband died, I became acutely aware of the absolute necessity of continuing to take time to build loving and intimate relationships. From my closet experience, I knew that God was with me, but I desperately needed physical connections. During those long, dark days after Dick's death, my doorbell rang day and night. I had friends hug me, pray with me, buy my groceries, bring meals, and walk with me. A group of friends rented a bus and traveled to the funeral from Lethbridge, Alberta, to Kelowna, British Columbia, at the worst time of the year—the week before Christmas. When they all showed up at my door with flowers, hugs, kisses, and prayers, my soul felt it as a healing balm. These friends were a tangible, earthly expression of a perfect, heavenly love.

We are created and designed for connection, but, sadly, in our quest to find pleasure, fulfillment, and meaning, many of us become lost and lonely.

CONNECTING WITH ONE ANOTHER

Connection takes place when we feel heard, seen, and not judged. It's not about having hundreds of friends on Facebook, presenting only the good selfies during our exotic vacations, and displaying our accomplishments and the fun and frivolous things we do. It is about becoming honest and vulnerable with each other. Vulnerability is a frightening process, because it means opening up our hopes, dreams, and weaknesses to the possibility they may be abused, rejected, or trampled on. But without vulnerability, there can be no intimacy.

Connection takes place when we feel heard, seen, and not judged.

I am writing this book in the middle of a glorious summer here in Kelowna, British Columbia. I do have a lot of acquaintances, but over the years I have recognized the vital importance of close and trusted friends. One magical evening, I had two special friends over for an evening barbecue on our deck. We shared a pleasant meal and good conversation. And then it got dark. In the glow of the candlelight and in the soft summer breeze, we dared to step into honesty and vulnerability. We talked about our growing-up years, our disappointments, failures, and hurts. Things our parents did and did not do. Lost opportunities and even some regrets. Soon some candles burned out and, looking at our watches, we knew it was time to end the night and step back into reality. As we hugged and waved goodnight, I knew that our vulnerability and candour had only drawn us closer. My soul was complete to overflowing.

FULFILL YOUR SOUL

Connections don't just happen. They require vulnerability, intentional effort, and time. Let's look at some things that might be holding us back from connecting with God and each other.

1. I'm on Facebook, Twitter, LinkedIn, and Pinterest, and I enjoy what they have to offer. But we all have to recognize that pictures and words behind a screen will never give us the energy an honest and intimate relationship will provide. Evaluate your time on social media. Is it realistic and healthy, or do you need to spend more time connecting with people in the real world?

2. Loneliness is a cruel word, and even harder when lived out. But we need to get honest with our feelings and recognize we are not designed to live this way. Ask yourself:
   - *Am I really alone? Or are there people I could reach out to but haven't made an effort?*
   - *What have I done to create relationships? Have I put myself out there to let people know I need a friend?* One of the best ways to find and meet like-minded people is to get out and do the things you love. Before you know it, you will find those wonderful people along the way.
   - *Have I joined a small group where I kept showing up?* Consistency is important, to give people a chance to get to know you better.

3. Vulnerability can be a terrifying word. To become vulnerable, we have to believe we are worthy of love and nurture a relationship where there is trust. The best trust relationship we will ever have is with our Abba Father. He is the one with the perfect plan for our lives, the one who wants us to spend time with him experiencing his extravagant love for us. When we feel loved, we gain the confidence to become vulnerable.

4. We lose out on joy when we are too busy chasing what we don't have. We need to stop running after illusions and enjoy these kinds of moments:

Your children giggling in the back seat.
Watching the full moon come up each month.
Licking an ice cream cone.
Dangling your feet in the lake.
Watching a long putt.
Creating something, then admiring the beauty of it.
Growing flowers and watching them bloom.
Reading a captivating book.

5. You are enough. It's hard to get that from our heads into our hearts and make it stick. Those short-lived feelings of being enough are so fleeting. How do we make them stick?

- Connect with people who will affirm you.
- Find someone to mentor you, who will constantly remind you that you are enough and you're not alone.
- Read books on love. I highly suggest John Ortberg's book *Love Beyond Reason: Moving God's Love from Your Head to Your Heart.*[41]
- Do something you love doing, and spend time getting better at it. When we finally acquire a skill we enjoy and we know we are good at it, it gives us confidence in other areas of our lives.
- Know that you are a work-in-progress and that God is always shaping, refining, and making you more beautiful from the inside out. But in this moment, you are perfect the way you are.

S.T.O.P. AND ASK GOD TO HELP YOU
FULFILL YOUR SOUL

BEGIN BY ASKING: *How can I let go of my shame?*

S-Scripture: "Those who look to him for help will be radiant with joy" (Psalm 34:5 NLT).

T-Thanksgiving: "Oh, I want to be radiant! Thank you, God, that my radiance and joy come from you. Thank you that I can ask you for help in any situation."

O-Observation: It's even shameful to admit that I might have shame. But I do recognize that we are all sinners, and we all suffer with shame. I don't want any hindrances in my life to stop me from living fully alive and completely fulfilled. In order to do that, I know I have to embrace vulnerability and acknowledge I have shame.

P-Prayer: "Abba Father, thank you for loving me just the way I am. Thank you that when you hung on the cross, you poured your blood over my sins and covered my shame. Because of the "joy set before him he endured the cross, scorning its shame" (Hebrews 12:2 NIV). This tells me that after we endure shame, there is joy. Father, please help me to release all my shame. I want to experience the joy of being free and vulnerable so that I can reach out and connect deeply and intimately with you and other people. Help me let go of any distractions or barriers that are hindering my journey to be all that you designed me to be. Thank you. Amen."

CHAPTER 6

FULFILLMENT THROUGH ENCOURAGING ONE ANOTHER

You're the Best

Encouragement is awesome. It (can) actually change the course of another person's day, week, or life.
—CHUCK SWINDOLL

THIS TIME IT was different.

Every summer, I take my staff to a unique restaurant. Over a splendid meal in a conducive setting, my girls engage in authentic and meaningful conversations—laced with bouts of laughter. But this would be my last summer meal with these women I deeply valued. They had worked for me and supported me during some difficult and challenging periods. In a few months, I would retire from a twenty-one-year career as controller for a VW and Audi franchise. I'd enjoyed those years, and I knew I would miss the daily camaraderie.

The magical summer evening in the Okanagan Valley matched the ambiance of the tables tucked away among flowers, plants, and beautifully decorated tables on the restaurant patio. We took time ordering our favorite meals, catching up on our families, children, pets, and upcoming summer activities. Before we ordered dessert, I asked each girl to find a glass we could use for toasting. Then I began.

I invited all the girls to raise their glasses for a toast. Then I faced Jeanne, and as I looked directly at her I said, "Jeanne, you're the best." From the puzzled looks on everyone's faces I knew they were wondering, *What has Jeanne done to deserve a toast?* I continued. "Jeanne, you're the best because you have been with me a long time, you perform your work well, and you always come to work on time. You're the best because you are a team player, always ready to help others, and you treat people with respect. You're the best because you help out even when it's not part of your job, and because you are always kind, gracious, and quick to laugh."

I stopped and looked around the table. The rest of the women were focused intently on what I was saying, so I continued. I expounded a few more superlatives about this amazing woman, and then had everyone raise their glass in a toast to Jeanne. Next, I turned my attention to each of the other gals and repeated this process until every woman at the table had heard me say, "You're the best." Last, I toasted my assistant, who had worked by my side for over seven years. We both fought back tears while I expressed the overflowing list of her most beautiful qualities: resilience, loyalty, attention to detail, and the relentless pursuit to perform perfectly. As we pulled out our Kleenex packets, we sniffled and tried to hide our deep emotions. But judging by the pictures on my iPhone, I know this was a special moment in time.

My gifts to these incredible women were simple words of encouragement. The cost? Honesty, vulnerability, and truth spoken with love and authenticity. Yet I knew that the memories and meaningful affirmation evoked in all of their lives was priceless. I believe loving and honest words have the same effect as stated in the Bible: "Kind words are like honey—enjoyable and healthful" (Proverbs 16:24 TLB).

Our souls long for words that validate our existence and worth. Words spoken over three thousand years ago still have the same power today they did then. "Words kill, words give life; they're either poison or fruit—you choose" (Proverbs 18:21 MSG).

Growing up, I remember chanting, "Sticks and stones may break my bones, but words will never hurt me." But the fact remains; words can hurt us deeply and crush our spirits. Alternatively, they hold the power to call out our goodness and breathe new life into our restless and hungry souls. In *Your Best Life Now*, Joel Osteen gives quite a challenge: "We should never speak a negative, destructive word toward anybody, especially toward people over whom we have authority or influence. Just because you have your own business or supervise a large number of employees doesn't give you the right to talk down to them and make them feel badly about themselves. Quite the contrary! God is going to hold you accountable for what you say to those individuals under your authority, and He is going to judge you by a stricter standard. You should go out of your way to speak positive words that build up and encourage."[42]

It is quite startling that when I "go out of my way" to speak loving words, I can make a person stand taller, feel more beautiful, and walk more confidently. Or I can crush their self-esteem and cause them to question their abilities. That's a big responsibility.

ENCOURAGEMENT UNLEASHES GOD'S GOODNESS

God has put us on this earth to help one another. One of the most practical and powerful ways to unleash God's goodness is through words of encouragement. The Bible tells us, "Therefore encourage one another and build each other up, just as in fact you are doing" (1 Thessalonians 5:11 NIV). The world is a harsh place these days. Reading the news about terrorism, planes disappearing, ISIS destroying ancient artifacts, mall shootings, and marriages disintegrating can make us cynical and hopeless. Oftentimes people cry out, "So where is God in all this mess?" Despite what we see and hear, we need to remind each other of God's promises and his unchanging goodness and faithfulness.

Underneath the messy, ugly rubble of our lives, God's goodness is alive and well and longing to be acknowledged and released. As Christians we have received God's grace through the forgiveness of our sins and past messes, and he has restored our dignity. We have been given a second chance and are now alive with new motives, passions, and goodness that need to be shared and passed along. When we do this, we obey God's command to love one another, and we breathe new life into another person. Through encouraging words, we pass along the very breath of hope that is available to us through the power of the Holy Spirit. In his book *Connecting*, Larry Crabb boldly declares, "The central calling of community is to connect, not to disrupt, to release something powerful from within one person into the life of another that calls for the goodness in another's heart."[43]

One of the most practical and powerful ways to unleash God's goodness is through words of encouragement.

During the last five years of my mother's life I discovered the power of transformation in a very unusual and practical way. My precious mother was diagnosed with a precancerous blood disease called myelodysplasia, a disorder where the bone marrow fails to produce sufficient quantities of normal blood cells. There is no medication to heal this condition, and the main treatment is blood transfusions. For a period of five years in three-week cycles, my sister, Brigitte, my new husband, Jack, and I accompanied mother to the hospital for blood transfusions. Within two days after each transfusion, we could always tell what kind of blood she received. We'd utter a sigh of relief when she received "good" blood. Her skin color looked healthier, her eyes were brighter, she spoke with new energy, and she felt refreshed in spirit. Conversely, there were also times when it was obvious she got weak blood. She was listless, tired, and pale, and she struggled to get out of bed in the morning.

What a powerful example of how Christ's goodness, flowing through us, has the influence and power to pour new life into one another. Our loving words can put new color into someone's face, add a spring to their step, and re-energize them with hope. We can also build up their courage and instill new hope through several other ways.

Strengthen by Consolation.

Encouragement is not flattery, nor merely nice compliments. I'm being selfish when I use it to make myself feel good about making someone else feel better. Encouragement involves a sincere motive to love someone, refresh their joy, and strengthen their spiritual walk with Jesus Christ. The word encourage in the Greek language is the verb *parakaleō*, which means "to console, to encourage, and strengthen by consolation, to comfort; to strengthen and to call to one's side, call for, summon."[44] There is nothing soft about this word. We are called to walk alongside them, offering them new strength by listening to their hardships, pain, or grief, then supplying encouragement.

When Jesus left this world, he told his disciples he was leaving us a *parakaleo*, a comforter. Someone to walk alongside us and help us. "But when the Father sends the Comforter instead of me—and by the Comforter I mean the Holy Spirit—he will teach you much, as well as remind you of everything I myself have told you" (John 14:26 TLB). So when someone is struggling and needs consoling, we get to be their Jesus, walking alongside them, giving them words of hope and strength to lift them out of their dark circumstances.

Often I take women out for what I call an encouragement lunch. One of those friends is my dear Linda.[45] A single mom with a demanding day job, Linda is very involved in her church while also completing an online master's of administration course. When she feels overwhelmed and tired, I can't fix her packed schedule or lighten her workload. But I do what I can. I tell her, "Linda, I am going to take you for an encouragement lunch next week." Linda is a beautiful daughter of our Lord, and she knows the Bible from cover to cover. But sometimes we just need someone to call us aside, listen to our struggles and remind us: "Jehovah God is our Light and our Protector. He gives us grace and glory. No good thing will he withhold from those who walk along his paths" (Psalm 84:11 TLB). We need to remember that our God is Jehovah-Jireh, "The Lord will provide," and he is also Jehovah-Rohi, "The Lord is my shepherd." When Linda and I connect face to face over a delicious lunch and remind ourselves of the goodness of our God, she is strengthened and we both are encouraged. We become motivated, moving into the day with a new bounce in our steps and smiles on our faces.

Build Each Other Up.

One of the best ways to help build a strong foundation in someone's life is to get to know them, earn their respect, and then speak with truth and love. The Bible tells us we need each other and we must stay connected. "Let us not neglect our meeting together, as some people do, but encourage one another, especially now that the day of his return is drawing near" (Hebrews 10:25 NLT). The Greek word for build is *oikodomeō*, a verb meaning "to build up from the foundation, to restore by building, to rebuild, repair."[46]

When we encounter new and daunting challenges, we all need someone to link arms with us, help us let go of fear, and build up our courage. Ten years ago, I walked up to two incredible women and asked them, "Would you like to get together to study the Bible and hold each other accountable?" I was delighted and amazed by their eager and immediate response of "Yes, we're in." For over ten years, the three of us have met in each other's homes, and we continue to do so whenever we can. Our evenings start out with a light meal of soup, bread, cheese, and fruit, and then we treat ourselves to a sumptuous dessert. We take our time eating our meal while catching up on each other's victories, challenges, children, grandchildren, and where we are at in our spiritual journey. At the end of the meal we move over to the living room, where we pick up the study material we've been working on since our last meeting. We take turns leading the discussion, then arrive at the best part of the evening—building each other up through words of encouragement and prayer.

Over the years we've shared our sins, acknowledged our failures, and mourned the loss of our parents. Throughout these journeys, filled with difficulties, we've grieved with and prayed for each other. But we've also celebrated and shared the joys of many victories and accomplishments: writing books, furthering our education, taking on influential and rewarding leadership positions. These times of intimate connection have given me courage, consoled me through the death of my mother, celebrated the publication of several of my books, strengthened my character, and built my faith. In every aspect, they have fulfilled my soul. Through these evenings spent in close relationship, I believe we have lived out this command: "But you, dear friends, must build up your lives ever more strongly upon the foundation of our holy faith, learning to pray in power and strength of the Holy Spirit" (Jude 1:20 TLB). Let's face it. We need each other.

Unleash One Another's Gifts and Abilities.

Jack and I love to see people use the gifts and abilities that God has given them. Passion and joy, erupting in someone's life when they are doing exactly what they have been designed to do, is contagious to our own spirits. But sadly, how often do we hear someone say, "Oh I could never do that"? Every one of us is bestowed with gifts given to us from our Heavenly Father. "Every good and perfect gift is from above, coming down from the Father of the heavenly lights, who does not change like shifting shadows" (James 1:17 NIV). And our giftings are endless, as stated by Rick Warren in *The Purpose Driven Life*: "One of the most common excuses people give for not serving is 'I don't have any abilities to offer.' This is ludicrous. You have dozens, probably hundreds, of untapped, unrecognized, and unused abilities that are lying dormant inside you."[47]

Over the years, Jack and I have tapped many people on the shoulder and said things like, "I believe you have the gift of leadership."

Or, "You would do great leading the youth ministry."

"Your athletic skills can get you a scholarship into a certain university."

"You know how to create beautiful cupcakes. You should open up a business."

"You can bring a Bible story to life. Have you considered teaching grades 4–6?"

These bold and affirming statements have the power to direct a person onto a pathway that will fulfill their own soul while building up the church. The Bible explains why: "Why is it that he gives us these special abilities to do certain things best? It is that God's people will be equipped to do better work for him, building up the Church, the body of Christ, to a position of strength and maturity" (Ephesians 4:12 TLB).

Jack and I love our large, eclectic blended family, and we try to take a special interest in each of our grandchildren's lives. Our oldest grandson, Brendon, recently earned his bachelor's degree and is focusing on and exploring the next stage of his life. We may be a little biased, but of course we think Brendon is absolutely brilliant, handsome, loaded with abilities, and there is nothing he can't do. Apparently we aren't the only ones who think so. His next step was to attend the Fudan University in Shanghai to learn Mandarin. When he applied for scholarships, part of the process was obtaining letters of recommendation from his professors. Jack and I had the privilege to read one.

This professor took an inordinate amount of time outlining all of Brendon's abilities in detail. Through other brilliant superlatives, he captured the very essence of who Brendon is and brought to life all the goodness and brilliance stored in our grandson. This busy man took the time to build a future foundation for our grandson, and his initiative humbles me. As I write this chapter, Brendon is in Shanghai on a scholarship program, and I know that the professor's letter profoundly impacted Brendon's future. May we all take the time to write and speak words that help build others' strength and unleash God's goodness in our own lives.

BE A BARNABUS

We always remember the person who showed up just when we needed someone. When I think of an encourager in the Bible, the name Barnabas clearly comes to mind. He was called "Son of Encouragement," a Levite from the island of Cyprus well known for his encouragement. The Bible records it this way: "When the church at Jerusalem heard what had happened, they sent Barnabas to Antioch. When he arrived and saw this evidence of God's blessing, Barnabas was a good man, full of the Holy Spirit and strong in faith. And many people were brought to the Lord" (Acts 11:22–24 NLT).

I would love to be remembered as a "Woman of Encouragement." What would it take to follow Barnabas' example?

Be a good woman or man.

A good reputation does not happen overnight. I love the way author Priscilla Shirer describes it in *The Resolution for Women*. "A woman whose heart is full of gratitude and humility, who is certain of God's love for her, and who genuinely prizes the worth of others around her will release a steady stream of graciousness that will refresh others through her conversation, others will desire the joy of her company because they know she seeks their welfare and esteems them more highly than herself."[48] This is the kind of woman people will call on when they need encouragement.

Be a mentor.

Barnabas mentored Paul as he began working alongside the other teachers in Antioch, and he encouraged Paul in his preaching. The Bible tells us that Barnabas was full of the Holy Spirit and strong in his faith, and he passed these faith gifts and qualities along to Paul and the new converts. When people spoke negatively about Paul, Barnabas stood up for him and defended him. What a tremendous gift when someone believes in us and covers our back. We can all be a mentor to someone and encourage them to stay close to God, to stick it out in their marriages, reconcile broken relationships, and refresh their spirits.

Be a listener.

When we give people our ears, we offer them a sliver of life and time we can never retract. We make people feel loved, accepted, and valued when we listen without judgment or our own agenda. Barnabas was a kind person, and only kind people are unselfishly motivated to put someone else's feelings above their own. Listening with love is one of the most practical ways we can impart to others that they have self-worth and significance.

When we give people the gift of listening, we offer them a sliver of life and time we can never retract.

Be a reconciler.

Paul and Barnabas seriously disagreed about taking John Mark along on their return trip to Turkey. They went separate ways for a while, and there must have been moments of miscommunication, strife, and heavy hearts. But the Bible tells us that later they worked together, serving the church in Corinth (1 Corinthians 9:6 TLB), so they must have also shared words of encouragement, reconciliation, and love. "Anxious hearts are very heavy, but a word of encouragement does wonders!" (Proverbs 12:25 TLB). Because of the love and forgiveness we have received from Christ, each one of us has a responsibility in our areas of influence to be agents of reconciliation. Because of Christ in us, our words have the power to heal. "A word of encouragement heals the one who receives" (Proverbs 15:4 VOICE).

Was Barnabas a perfect man? Of course not. But the Bible records the lives of men such as Barnabas to show us what great things God can do through men and women who use their faith and gift of encouragement to build up the body of Christ.

FULFILL YOUR SOUL

Most of us can remember that defining moment when someone's words seemed to hug us like a warm blanket, lifted us out of darkness, or even changed the course of our life. Our souls can be refilled through a hug, smile, or a loving touch on the shoulder. And as we encourage others, we also feel uplifted and fulfilled. It's absolutely baffling how that works, but the Bible affirms this. "It is possible to give away and become richer! It is also possible to hold on too tightly and lose everything. Yes, the liberal man shall be rich! By watering others, he waters himself" (Proverbs 11:24–25 TLB).

Here are ways we can water others so that, in turn, our own souls will be fulfilled.

Loving and caring touch.

While Jesus walked on this earth, he constantly touched people, including untouchable lepers and a bleeding woman. Scientists have documented that human touch has the power to form closer bonds, heal, and lower heart rate and cortisol levels. It leads to emotional, physical, and cognitive improvements and is the best predictor of happiness, health, and longevity.[49] By a simple touch, we can water someone's soul and body. See the Study Guide for more conversation about appropriate touch.

Writing.

Throughout the New Testament, the epistles are filled with notes of encouragement to the young churches that were growing and learning to follow Jesus Christ. Our notes don't need to be that lengthy, but written words on a piece of paper have great power—a note, postcard, even just a sticky note to say, "I see you are going through a rough time and I care." You can refresh the soul of someone who's lonely and grieving, or someone who's discouraged about unemployment, wayward children, or a recent health diagnosis. Your simple, loving note can give them new hope.

Offering a hand.

When I felt overwhelmed at my workplace and someone said, "You look tired, can I help you?" it felt like I was given a life preserver. A helping hand in time of need brings life to someone's soul.

Offer to take a colicky baby, store someone's furniture, sew, cut grass, or do odd shopping jobs. You'll change their feelings of loneliness and despair to feelings of connectedness and fulfillment.

Showing up.

I love text messages, e-mails, and Facebook posts, and they definitely have their value and advantages. But not when I'm going through a crisis. This is the time to simply show up and offer words of comfort and hope. Psalm 34:18 says, "The Lord is close to those whose hearts are breaking," and often the Lord sends us in person on his behalf.

Forming your own "Barnabas Group."

F.B. Meyer (1847-1929), the great Bible teacher, pastor, and author of over forty books, once remarked that if he had his life to live over, he'd spend more time in the ministry of encouragement. Brainstorm with others to find ways to encourage people. It will bring you joy and open doors you never knew existed.

Our restless spirit longs to be affirmed, and encouragement is one of the best gifts in the world. It fulfills our soul, costs nothing, and yet is priceless.

S.T.O.P. AND ASK GOD TO HELP YOU
FULFILL YOUR SOUL

BEGIN BY ASKING: *What gift of encouragement can I give away?*

S-Scripture: "Therefore encourage one another and build each other up, just as in fact you are doing" (1 Thessalonians 5:11 NIV).

T-Thanksgiving: "Thank you, God, that because of the love and example of encouragement you gave mankind when you walked this earth, I am able to encourage others. Thank you that the Holy Spirit will give me everything I need when I step out in the faith of encouraging others."

O-Observation: There are so many needs and demands in the world, I hardly know where to begin. People are suffering with cancer, marriages blowing apart, and Christians struggling on their spiritual journey. God, where do I start? Some days it feels as useless as dropping a penny into the ocean. Yet I know the power of just the right word at the right time. I know that when I uplift others, my own soul will also be refreshed and refilled. This is an area of my life where I must never give up. I know it makes a difference.

P-Prayer: "God, help me be an encourager like Barnabas. I want to be known as a kind, godly person who helps others grow in their spiritual journey. Help me to see others' needs and then take the initiative to step out in faith and give the gift of encouragement at the right time. Open my eyes to see gifts and abilities that need to be unleashed in others, and then to have the courage to speak to them about their possible glorious and exciting future. Help me be a person of strength so I can build people up, stand up for them, and cover their backs when they need me. God, as I encourage others, please fill me with your love, so that peace and contentment ultimately satisfies my own soul. Thank you. Amen."

CHAPTER 7

FULFILLMENT THROUGH BEING KIND TO ONE ANOTHER

Love in Shoe Leather

Constant kindness can accomplish much. As the sun makes ice melt, kindness causes misunderstanding, mistrust, and hostility to evaporate.
—ALBERT SCHWEITZER (1875–1965)

THE TUMULTUOUS POST-REVOLUTIONARY ERA in France provides a spectacular theatrical setting for the movie *Les Misérables*. The year is 1815, and Jean Valjean is released from prison after nineteen years of hard labor for stealing a loaf of bread to feed his hungry family. But life continues to be cold and cruel, as his parole status hinders him from finding employment. He is hungry, rejected, and lonely. I saw this production twice on stage and once in the movie theatre, and still I cry my way through the scenes when Jean finally encounters compassion through the kind Bishop of Digne.

The bishop invites Jean to his supper table to feed his stomach, but also to offer a message of hope, kindness, and a warm bed. Overcome by temptation, Jean Valjean steals the bishop's silverware and slips into the dark night.

Stopped by a constable, Jean Valjean tries to weasel his way out of trouble. Alas, they throw him at the bishop's feet and Jean listens for the words that will condemn him to prison. Nothing prepared him for what he hears next. Instead of condemning and chastising Jean, the bishop extends radical kindness, even agreeing with Jean's claim that the bishop gave him the silver. I am always blindsided when the bishop turns around, reaches for more silver candlesticks standing on the table behind him and says, "But my friend, you left so early you forgot I gave you these also. Why would you leave the best behind?"

Jean Valjean expected prison. Instead, he received kindness. This is when I pull out the Kleenex. My human, selfish nature can barely comprehend that kind of extravagant, selfless kindness. Because of this great kindness, the ex-convict decides to turn his life around. Eventually he became mayor of a town in France and owner of a factory.

The word *kindness* sounds limpid, but in fact it is an action verb disguised as a noun and has nothing to do with weakness or lack of conviction. Radio host Adrian Rogers described kindness as "love in shoe leather."[50] This is a picture of walking in tenderness and love to extend kindness with strength and courage. Furthermore, it is important to distinguish it from "being nice." Being nice may involve being cooperative, agreeable, or pleasant, but it doesn't cost us much in terms of time or effort. Kindness digs down deep and calls for action, growth, and "shoe-leather strength."

Kindness digs down deep and calls for action, growth, and "shoe-leather strength."

For many people, kindness is not the default response. "Our brains have a 'negativity bias,' which predisposes us to fear-based, kindness-killing behaviors like rushing and defensiveness."[51] Our human, selfish, restless spirit is more prone to say, "I don't even have enough for myself, so how do you expect me to give my time or treasures away? Even though we may want to be kind, daily challenges are inevitable and rob us of whatever compassion we might have had when we got up that morning. There will always be drivers who don't know how to merge properly, aggravatingly slow line-ups, mean-spirited gossipers, and telemarketers who call during dinner hour. Many people are so intent on their daily to-do lists and agendas, they treat people like pawns on a chessboard.

I notice a decline in human kindness. Many young people don't bother to open doors or give up bus seats for the elderly. The seeming lack of respect betrays hearts that are empty and so self-focused there is no time to waste on anything that doesn't benefit them. People are so engaged with their phones, they don't take the time to look up and smile or say please and thank you. I was saddened and shocked by the research done by the University of Michigan, which explains that one of the reasons we have become so selfish and restless is because, "compared to thirty years ago, the average American now is exposed to three times as much non-work-related information. In terms of media content, this generation of college students grew up with video games, and research done by my colleagues at Michigan, is establishing that exposure to violent media numbs people to the pain of others."[52]

"We found the biggest drop in empathy after the year 2000," said Sara Konrath, a researcher at the U-M Institute for Social Research. "College kids today are about forty percent lower in empathy than their counterparts of twenty or thirty years ago, as measured by standard tests of this personality trait."[53]

When I read this, it broke my heart for all of mankind. This is not how Jesus intended us to live. The Greek word for "kindness" is *chréstotés* and denotes "the *Spirit-produced* goodness which meets the need and avoids human harshness."[54] This comes from the Greek root word *charis*, which is "grace." Kindness is a fruit of the spirit, which I believe is the most tender and yet strongest expression of God's love and grace to heal and comfort a lost and broken world.

KINDNESS DOES

Until I became a Christian, I didn't fully understand the power of sincere kindness motivated by God's love. My acts of kindness were generous gestures meant to appease my guilt or try to earn some brownie points. I did nice things. I bought painted rocks from the children in the neighborhood or sent a shoebox to Africa at Christmas. I did my share of knocking on doors collecting money for cancer or the Heart Fund. Now that I have a better grasp on how kindness can change someone's day or even life, I do it as a deliberate act, motivated sincerely to be more like Christ.

I am motivated to be kind because in the midst of my messy and broken life, Christ's kindness removed my ugly sin and gave me a second chance at a beautiful life. The Bible says it perfectly: "Once we, too, were foolish and disobedient. We were misled and became slaves to many lusts and pleasures. Our lives were full of evil and envy, and we hated each other. But—When God our Savior revealed his kindness and love, he saved us, not because of the righteous things we had done, but because of his mercy. He washed away our sins, giving us a new birth and new life through the Holy Spirit" (Titus 3:3–5 NLT).

Think of what it cost Jesus to pour his kindness onto mankind. He took on God's wrath for you and me and ended up being betrayed, rejected, and beaten. He had to carry his own cross and watch as the Roman soldiers mockingly rolled dice to see who would get Jesus' clothes. I know that God's kindness has utterly transformed my life because of a free gift from his son Jesus Christ, so I need to take an honest inventory to see how I can express this gift to the rest of the world. Here are some examples of what Jesus did:

- He broke down barriers by getting close to the "unclean" lepers and did something for them no one else would do.
- He was kind to the despised Samaritans.
- He loved the children and treated them with deep tenderness.
- He looked upon the crowds with compassion. When they were hungry, he fed them.
- He never turned anyone away.
- He turned water into wine.
- He knew Judas was going to betray him, yet he was never cruel or unkind.
- He broke social barriers by talking to a Samaritan woman at the well in the middle of the day.

We may never heal anyone by the laying on of hands or turn water into wine, but we women have great influence in our homes, workplaces, and neighborhoods. By exuding a Holy Spirit resolve to be kind, we can literally change the emotional and moral temperature from tension to tenderness. It means making a grumpy person their favorite tuna salad sandwich when they least deserve it, or removing a bicycle from the driveway. It might compel you to pay a bill that was not your responsibility or stay late at the office to fix someone's mistake. But when Jesus infuses our hearts with the fruit of kindness, it gets poured out in the most beautiful, radical, and undeserving ways.

I am privileged to mentor a beautiful young woman who was a captain of the British Columbia division of the Salvation Army in Vernon, British Columbia. She exercises the gift of kindness through helping prostitutes. This is Ray's story of love in shoe leather.

> *The first time I saw Heather*, she was working on the street corner five blocks away from my apartment in inner-city Montreal. When I saw her she was dressed like a little schoolgirl, in uniform and pigtails standing on a street corner with her "wife." As I drove past Heather, God spoke to my soul that this woman and I were going to be good friends and that we would mutually impact each other's lives. Two weeks later on a Friday night, I met Heather while our group was finishing up our street ministry. Even though it was midnight we talked for another two hours, as much as one can when they are extremely high. Heather had been trafficked into prostitution when she was one month from turning twelve. When I met her she was thirty-eight.*
>
> *For the next five years, I journeyed with Heather through some amazingly brilliant moments and some extremely low points. She was HIV-positive, so we had regular doctor appointments to pick up her cocktail of medicine. On Mondays when she received her weekly check from her curator, I took her to a grocery store and taught her how to buy food within a budget. When she*

was released from prison, I was there to pick her up. When she was critically ill, I visited her in the hospital and then let her stay at my place so that I could cook her some healthy meals. Early one cold November morning, I picked her up along with her pet mouse from a home where she was living on a patio. Her client at the time would only let her in when he wanted sex. For a short period of time I took her to a Salvation Army safe house where she was off the streets, out of prostitution, clean, and happy. When she went back and forth into prostitution and drugs, I went looking for her on the streets. During the time I lived in Quebec, I made monthly visits to her boyfriend who was in prison.

My friend Heather is dead now. During our time together she became my sister. Her life, her person, her beauty, and her story impacted me in ways that are beyond description. The love and compassion that I felt for my friend motivated me to shower her with acts of kindness. At times it was extremely difficult, and often I had to make huge sacrifices. But through my friendship and journey with Heather I found something valuable and fulfilling. When we are kind and compassionate to one another that God not only fulfills our souls but our own lives are enriched beyond anything that we could ever imagine or hope for.[55]

POWER OF KINDNESS

I've witnessed how kindness can put a spring in someone's step or a glow in his or her cheeks. I was delighted and amazed when I discovered the healing powers of expressing and receiving kindness. The article, "The Healing Power of Kindness," in the *Huffpost Healthy Living*, outlines this enlightening research.

An extensive scientific literature review sponsored by Dignity Health and conducted by the Center for Compassion and Altruism Research and Education (CCARE) at Stanford University reveals a growing body of scientific evidence that indicates kindness holds the power to heal. We now know that this often overlooked, virtually cost-free remedy has a statistically significant impact on our physical health. For example, the positive effect of kindness is even greater than that of taking aspirin to reduce the risk of a heart attack or the influence of smoking on male mortality. And it doesn't even require a trip to the pharmacy.[56]

An apple a day may keep the doctor away, but an act of kindness can also improve our physical health. Until I discovered this research, I could not fully grasp the concept of the verse that says, "Be kind and good to others; then you will live safely here in the land and prosper" (Psalm 37:3 NLB).

This verse correlates with the word *prosper* in 3 John 1:2, when it refers to prospering in health. Kindness is one of the most pleasurable human actions, and now I see that it is also one of the healthiest things we can do for others and ourselves. When we feel healthy, those positive feelings release nutrients that increase our creativity, and we are more optimistic and have a happier outlook on life. It evokes feelings of abundance rather than scarcity. It builds a stronger immune system and decreases feelings of depression and helplessness. When we are kind to each other as the Bible commands, we feel more connected to the rest of the world.

Our restless nature and scarcity mentality wants to hoard and accumulate more, to make us feel richer, stronger, and self-sufficient. But in God's glorious plan for humankind, he has something radically different in mind. He wants us to pour out to others so he can refill us. "Feed the hungry! Help those in trouble! Then your light will shine out from the darkness, and the darkness around you shall be as bright as day. And the Lord will guide you continually, *and satisfy you with all good things, and keep you healthy too;* and you will be like a well-watered garden, like an ever-flowing spring" (Isaiah 58:10–11 TLB, italics mine).

It takes both wisdom and heart to recognize different types of needs and just what kind of assistance is called for. But these kinds of deliberate actions are not simple random acts of kindness; they reflect life marked by the infusion of the Holy Spirit and longing to pour God's love onto a needy and hungry world. Mysteriously, we are the ones who end up being satisfied and flourishing like a well-watered garden.

IT TAKES TIME TO BE KIND

Each year, I pray for God to impress on me two words that will define the year. In 2014, one of the words God gave me was *kindness*. I admit, the word *kindness* stretched my spiritual muscles and made me I realize I was not much better than the people around me. We are all under pressure, rushing to get somewhere and do more, leaving no margin for kindness.

Six weeks before my mother died, while she was a patient in a loving and compassionate environment, the Hospice House in Kelowna, British Columbia, I witnessed and experienced the selfless and sacrificial kindness of people who care for the dying. My heart was gripped, and I discovered I needed deeper compassion for those who are struggling in this world. During the endless hours I spent beside my mother's bedside or wheeling her around the complex, I noticed that the most meaningful gifts were friends stopping by with hugs. I was aware that they, also, had chosen to carve out time in their busy lives to enter a place where the atmosphere silently screamed death. Yet they showed up.

Throughout those somber hours at Hospice House, I keenly observed nurses and trusted friends who displayed love in shoe leather. I saw how their kindness was the strongest, yet most tender, expression toward those dealing with life's lonely and painful seasons. It made me dig deep into my own soul. This verse also helped recalibrate my kindness plumb line: "If someone has enough money to live well and sees a brother or sister in need but shows no compassion—how can God's love be in that person?" (1 John 3:17 NLT). I always thought my heart was filled with God's love, but I had a lot to learn. In the midst of juggling extreme pressure at my workplace, trying to be a good wife and mother, meeting writing and speaking deadlines, and watching my mother die, I knew I was still in "kindness boot camp." God was showing me what kindness really meant.

I became acutely aware that it takes time to:

- Give someone a break, when it's the last thing you want to do.
- Listen to the same story even when you're tired and want to go home.
- Make an intentional effort to begin a conversation, such as asking a grumpy cashier, "So what kind of a day are you having?"
- Have patience with a cranky, elderly senior.
- Help someone fix a mistake.
- Go for a walk with a grieving neighbor.
- Help someone move.
- Sit with a dying friend or parent.

Kindness is not being a doormat or acquiescing to uncomfortable or unrealistic demands. Kindness is a sincere desire to allow the Holy Spirit to shape our hearts like Jesus, overflowing with compassion for a hurting world. The Bible puts it this way: "Since you have been chosen by God who has given you this new kind of life, and because of his deep love and concern for you, you should practice tenderhearted mercy and kindness to others" (Colossians 3:12 TLB). This Scripture is a loud command, not just a nice suggestion. To follow the example of Jesus Christ, we need to make time to show up. It means setting aside our selfish nature, opening our heart of compassion, and stepping into our leather shoes.

KINDNESS LEAVES A LEGACY

Among my treasured possessions, I still have letters dated from 1973 to 1975 between me and Mother Teresa at her address at St. Vincent's Home in Agra, India. During that period, I was president of the Kinette Club of Penticton, British Columbia where I initiated and supervised the adoption of Miss Nirmala Mary to St. Vincent's Home. Although this was a period before I was a Christian, I knew in my heart Mother Teresa was an extraordinary woman displaying extravagant kindness. After reading part of her biography, I have a better understanding of her determination and passion when she says, "As to my calling, I belong to the world. As to my heart, I belong entirely to the Heart of Jesus . . . God still loves the world and He sends you and me to be His love and His compassion to the poor."[57]

Mother Teresa's compassion took her from the poorest of the poor in the slums in Calcutta to recipient of the Medal of Freedom from President Reagan on June 20, 1985.[58] She left an unforgotten legacy.

Not many of us will find our Calcutta, but my husband, Jack, shares a story about his father who found his Calcutta in the mines of Northern Ontario.

> *My father found his Calcutta at his place of employment in the engineering department of Frood Mine, which was a part of the International Nickel Company, Sudbury, Ontario. I will never forget my first day at the mine. Dad left his office and was waiting for me at the base of the head frame to shake my hand and wish me God's blessing before I stepped into the cage to the underground. Talk about an initiation into manhood! When the miners learned I was Fred's son, they regaled me with stories of my dad stopping to listen, advise, and encourage as he went about making inspections. Dad never forgot that we had been brought to faith in Christ through the kindness of Christ. The memory of my parents' kindness and the kindness that was, in turn, demonstrated to them remains a lasting legacy inspiring us even today.*
>
> *Kindness is a wise use of the heart. It is motivated and inspired by our reflection upon the kindness of God our Savior. Kindness leaves a beautiful, permanent legacy.[59]*

FULFILL YOUR SOUL

For almost thirty years, my Calcutta has been the broken, hurting, and lost women in North America. It's not as gritty and sacrificial as Mother Teresa's, but it requires me to give my all. Ministering to hurting women leaves me deliciously exhausted. But it fulfills me beyond money, a new pair of shoes, the most scrumptious banquet, or a new car. If we want to experience fulfillment and happiness, we need to pour compassion and kindness out on others. A portion of *Your Best Life Now* explains it succinctly:

Many people are unhappy and are not experiencing life to its fullest because they have closed their hearts to compassion. They are motivated by only what they want and what they think they need. They rarely do anything for anybody else unless they have an ulterior goal in mind. They are self-involved and self-centered. But if you want to experience God's abundant life, you must get your focus off yourself and start taking time to help other people. You must exhibit and express God's love and goodness wherever you go. You must be a person of compassion.[60]

Here are some ways we can pour kindness out to one another, and live the abundant life we were designed to enjoy.

1. One of the things that put a smile on my face is paying for the meal of the person behind me when I go through a fast-food drive-through. Try it sometime, and experience the thrill of knowing you made someone happy that day.

2. Perhaps you'll soon be in a crowded restaurant and notice the haggard faces of a family in a booth near you. Why not slip them a note saying you will pray for them, or maybe even pick up their dinner tab? When you see their faces light up, your heart will glow with fulfillment.

3. Evangelist and international speaker Joyce Meyer tells stories of how she goes through her closet to find things she can give away and bless people. It gives her tremendous joy when she expresses this kindness to women who don't have as much as she does. Why not go into your closet and pull out anything you haven't worn for two years, and give it to someone you know who needs it, or to a trusted charity organization? I know your spirit will rise up with fresh joy.

4. A number of years ago, I prepared a memory jar for my daughter. I spent hours going back in my mind through fun, meaningful, and adventurous memories of my daughter's growing-up years. Each memory took me back to those beautiful events, bringing a smile to my face. Writing out each memory on a piece of paper and then tucking them into a jar filled my own heart. The best

part was watching my daughter open the jar, read the memories, and laugh or cry with joy.

5. Listen to the tone of your voice. Is it sharp, irritated, or blunt? Being kind and compassionate is strength and joy only when you are honest with your own feelings. When you are always being "nice" and not expressing your own thoughts, you'll feel powerless, fatigued, and resentful. You need to take time to be kind to yourself also, identifying your toxic relationships, expressing your true feelings, and spending time doing what you love.

So, why should we be kind? As Plato said a very long time ago, "Be kind, for everyone you meet is fighting a hard battle." Many people feel terrible about themselves and their lives. But kindness is contagious; it impacts their circumstances, while fulfilling yours. Kindness takes time and courage. Let's be the best version of ourselves and be kind to everyone we meet.

S.T.O.P. AND ASK GOD TO HELP YOU FULFILL YOUR SOUL

BEGIN BY ASKING: *How can I become a kinder person?*

S-Scripture: "If someone has enough money to live well and sees a brother or sister in need but shows no compassion—how can God's love be in that person?" (1 John 3:17 NLT).

T-Thanksgiving: "Thank you, God, that you have a plan for all of us to live a fulfilling and glorious life. Thank you that your lavish love is poured out freely and generously so that all mankind can enjoy your extravagant benefits."

O-Observation: Sometimes it's very difficult to be kind. People are rushing, being inconsiderate, rude, and even mean. But the Scripture above states it clearly: if I lack compassion, I don't have God's love in me. I need to understand that people may be unkind because they are lonely, hurting, or are having a horrible day. Every day, I need God to fill me up with huge doses of his love, so I can pour it out selflessly and generously.

P-Prayer: "God, I want to be known for being the kindest person anyone has ever met. Reveal any insecurity in me that derails me from taking responsibility for my lack of kindness. Allow your love to heal me by revealing my critical and judgmental spirit. I want to see the world through your eyes of compassion, and to bring hope and kindness to my Calcuttas. Help me remember that the world will know you when I allow your love to be revealed through acts of kindness. Thank you that when I am obedient to this command, you will fill my soul with fresh joy and renewed faith. Amen."

CHAPTER 8

FULFILLMENT THROUGH HONORING ONE ANOTHER

Rewards for Honor

*A man that loves and cherishes his woman
and his family is a man of honor.*
—WAYNE CHIRISA

I KNOW WHAT HONOR feels like. I clearly remember the ecstasy, joy, and pride I experienced when I received medals for the highest achievement in twelfth-grade English. I'd sacrificed teenage dates and popular skating nights, instead laboring through Shakespeare and compiling dreaded poems. So I reveled in my well-deserved reward.

I still get choked up when I see others being honored, because I know how it feels. Each year when I watch the CNN HERO presentation, I'm moved with admiration, listening to the heroes' stories of unthinkable achievements.

HONOR

It amazes me that God desires to honor us. Psalm 8:5 says, "And yet you have made him a little lower than the angels and placed a crown of glory and honor upon his head" (TLB). In this verse, the Hebrew word for honor is *hadar,* which means magnificence, beauty, excellence, glory, majesty, and favor. That is what God wants to do for you and me—to pour goodness, favor, and reward into our lives. I love the way Joel Osteen clarifies this. "We do not receive favor because of who or what we are. It's not because we're something special on our own merit, or that we deserve to be treated so. Nor is it because we're better than anybody else. No, you will often receive preferential treatment simply because your Father is the King of kings, and his glory and honor spill over onto you." [61]

As a mother and stepmother, I catch glimpses of this delight. I love my children and grandchildren simply because they are mine and because God gave them to me as the best gift on earth. I love their smiles of sheer gratitude when they receive a reward for making a good choice or succeeding at a difficult task. In the same way, God loves to lavish us with his love and favor us with his goodness. Most of us love this verse because it's all about us receiving favor and rewards. Our restless nature always desires more good rewards. But there is another side to this equation.

HONOR YOUR MOTHER AND FATHER

After I began my personal relationship with Jesus, I found a verse in the Bible that shook me to the core. "Honor your father and mother. This is the first of God's Ten Commandments that ends with a promise. And this is the promise: that if you honor your father and mother, yours will be a long life, full of blessings" (Ephesians 6:2–3 TLB). I didn't want to be obedient to this verse because it meant I had to change my behavior. Of course I wanted the rewards of blessings, but I didn't want to honor my father and mother. The Greek word for honor in this passage is *timaō*, which means to prize, fix the value upon, revere, honor, or value. I struggled to grasp the truth that I would have to show them my highest respect.

As a teenager, I was horribly disrespectful to my parents. I thought they were out of touch with reality. They never seemed to listen to my ideas or applaud my successes. My dad angered me with his harsh, unrealistic rules. I felt hurt because my mother wouldn't make an effort to understand me or listen to the longings of my heart. Consequently, over time I defied all their demands, rebelled against family values, and chose to do life my way. But after I became a Christian I knew that if I wanted to experience the blessings of God in my life, I needed to change. You see, God wants to honor me, but I have to do my part.

I realize I am not the only one who struggles with this command to honor our parents. Many children suffer life-long trauma from abuse inflicted on them by their parents. Words were spoken that killed their self-worth and creativity and left them bereft of any value or confidence. Physical abuse imprinted on their spirits the idea that they are worthless and will never amount to anything. They experienced emotional indifference that shouted, "I don't value you enough to spend time with you or support you."

As a mentor, Bible teacher, and speaker, I have to grapple with these realities when I encounter women who struggle with these issues. Because of what I learned about honoring my parents, I can share biblical truths and personal insights.

God's commands are always for our own good, and he wants life to go well for us. Even when we don't agree with or are baffled by a challenge, Scripture cannot be interpreted from our limited human understanding. We must allow the breath of the Holy Spirit to guide us into truth and help us live out the correct application in each instance. Learning to be obedient to God starts by learning to be obedient and respectful to our parents. The family is the backbone of society, and home is where we learn how to love and communicate, as well as how to manage money. We learn lessons in acceptance and conflict resolution.

Learning to be obedient to God starts by learning to be obedient and respectful to our parents.

Too often I hear, "Well, I don't have to put up with that. I don't deserve to be treated that way." In this age of entitlement, we might feel that way. But I learned that by honoring my parents, I was in fact honoring God.

Once I grasped this concept, I showed my parents respect simply by not talking back or starting arguments. Instead of exploding with exasperation when we disagreed, I asked God to give me grace to see their point of view. I had to learn patience. They also had wounds and insecurities and were working to overcome abuse they experienced in their growing-up years. They were just like me, trying to figure out how to live the very best life.

But for some, the abuse is severe, and it means setting boundaries for limited contact, the occasional Skype call, or brief visit. Still others of you may have to let your parents live their lives, so you can live yours in peace. Whatever the circumstance, we all have to find that place where we know we have done our part to the best of our knowledge and ability.

Honor Your Parents because it Honors God

Some cultures around the world like those found in Asia and Europe uphold the value of honoring parents and elderly family members better than our North American culture. The only time most of us make intentional efforts to honor them is a one-day celebration on Mother's Day and Father's Day. That's not enough. As I mentor women, I give them some guidelines for how to truly honor their parents.

- *Honor them in spite of how you feel.* Honor them because you are in fact honoring God. The story of Joseph being tempted and seduced by Potiphar's wife (Genesis 39:3–9) is a great example of how we must respond to encounters that have the potential to make us say or do sinful acts. Joseph refused the sexual advances from Potiphar's wife saying, "How can I do such a wicked thing as this? It would be a great sin against God" (Genesis 39:9 TLB). His response came out of a place of desiring to honor God despite temptation that might have caused him to sin. In the same way, when we are tempted to be cruel to our parents to make them pay for any injustices we feel, we need to stop and view them as God's creations. If we sin against them, we are sinning against God. Keep in mind that honoring God pleases him and will ultimately provide blessings in our life.

- *Confrontation may be good, but it must be done with a right heart.* It must be done with love and grace for the sake of the other person—not for our sake. I often advise women for whom a face-to-face confrontation is unrealistic; to write a loving letter to their mother or father, expressing whatever pain or injustice is occurring in their lives. I always ask to review the letter before it is sent. The letter must not be written in a spirit of anger, retaliation, or being right, but rather, out of a heart of love and grace. Oftentimes the letters are never sent, because the simple process of writing the letter diffuses anger and negative emotions.
- *Expect that they may never give you the love you are looking for.* This was very hard for me to accept. Once I forgave my parents for not loving me the way I needed to be loved, I was able to accept their actions and behaviors in a completely different light. I believe a large amount of our pain and anger comes from not being loved the way we need our parents to love us. They are also imperfect people, and we have to accept the reality that their behavior may never change.
- *Honor them because they deserve it.* You might say, "Well my parents don't deserve my respect because they did a horrible job raising me." That is our normal human response. But I agree with this quote I read on a website: "Our parents resemble the Creator, since they were God's partners in the creation of the child. They also represent God in the life of the small child, functioning as primary caregiver and teacher. A person should recognize that his parents are the cause of his life in the world and it is therefore proper to love and respect them."[62]
- *Pray for wisdom and humility as to how you should honor your parents.* "Pride lands you flat on your face; humility prepares you for honors" (Proverbs 29:23 MSG). We selfish humans struggle with considering others better than ourselves, so we need the Holy Spirit to guide our thoughts, words, and actions. Great steps you can take toward preparing your heart for honor are humbling

yourself on your knees and confessing to your Heavenly Father that this is too big or hurtful to handle alone.

- *Don't react; respond.* When one of your parents says something hurtful or ruins another Thanksgiving dinner or birthday celebration, your initial tendency is to react in frustration. But you must stop, breathe, bite your tongue, and choose your words carefully before they slip out of your mouth. The Bible says, "Your own soul is nourished when you are kind; it is destroyed when you are cruel" (Proverbs 11:17 TLB).
- *Establish healthy boundaries.* While God expects us to honor our parents, he never expects us to act in an ungodly manner that could cause us to sin or disobey his commands. You may need an accountability partner or your husband to help you set healthy boundaries. My husband helped me to honor my mother by setting boundaries based on respect rather than guilt. He taught me how and when to say no, laced with love and grace. He helped me refocus my frustrations and realign my expectations so I would not be hurt and frustrated. When we seek to honor God first, he gives us the wisdom to have a strong voice and establish healthy boundaries.

Once I grasped the concept that by honoring my parents, I was in fact honoring God, I changed my words, expectations, and behaviors. Soon it overflowed into other areas of my life. Now I treat janitors and airline attendants differently. I take the time to talk to cashiers and look them in the eye. I tip the boys who clean my golf clubs and ask the tired clerk, "So how is your day going so far?" I try to make people feel they are important to me, and by doing so I am richly blessed.

When we seek to honor God first, he gives us the wisdom to have a strong voice and establish healthy boundaries.

HONOR ONE ANOTHER

The only way for me to honor my parents and all who God places in my life is to learn how to be obedient to honor God first. I love the way John Bevere clarifies this in his book *Honor's Reward*. "Enduring honor is found only in valuing Him above anything or anyone else. We are to value, esteem, respect, and reverence Him above anyone or anything. We dishonor Him if we value anyone or anything above Him. He is the Great King; He is worthy to receive all our respect, not just a portion. To God alone does our honor transcend to worship."[63]

This does not come naturally. It has to be learned. It became easier as I became more obedient to God and honored people he placed in my life. The Bible says we should be "asking that the way you live will always please the Lord and honor him, so that you will always be doing good, kind things for others, while all the time you are learning to know God better and better" (Colossians 1:10 TLB).

God gave me opportunity to honor him and "one another" in 2008 when I met Larry and Janet Dieno. Janet is a petite, energetic woman with a smile that lights up a room. I came to love this beautiful couple when they attended my study class on the topic of *30 Days to a No-Regrets Life*. We had lively discussions and much laughter, while learning many practical steps toward living without regret. We were all shocked when, in April of 2012, their world was shattered and our words were put to the test. I joined "Team Save Janet" after she suffered a ruptured brain aneurysm. Here is how Larry describes that journey:

> It took me two attempts to get this marriage thing right. My first relationship was built on seeing the other person as a means to gaining something we wanted. Often what we wanted was something materialistic or self-serving. Sometimes we masked those desires in "It'll be good for the kids." Or, "We'll pay for it later, no problem." Later, there certainly was a problem.
>
> I was fooling myself in my marriage and in my relationship with God. I went to church, even took the kids and sometimes the

wife. Now I realize I was going more out of guilt and fear than with a grateful heart ready to praise my Father. As that marriage broke down, my focus shifted to my children. Raising my three daughters taught me humility and forced me to look for positives instead of the usual negatives. It showed me that loving with genuine affection is more powerful than guilt or fear.

God brought me my true love when I least expected it. I watched the way Janet loved her kids and sacrificed for them. It was mind-blowing to see how they loved her back. It made me want that! Not in a self-serving way, but in a way that God could change my heart.

Janet and I have been married for twelve years now. These years were not without their challenges but built on Romans 12:10 (NLT) that says: "Love each other with genuine affection, and take delight in honoring each other." I can't say we really understood this verse and read it daily or had it posted on our fridge. We just learned to live it and continue to do so today. By taking delight in honoring each other and truly loving each other with genuine affection we were able to overcome obstacles that would have demolished most relationships. We overcame raising five teenagers in a blended family. We overcame legal battles with ex-spouses, family health issues, financial hurdles, and career changes. All of that led to the greatest challenge of all when Janet suffered a ruptured brain aneurysm. Without that solid foundation of love between Janet and I and our children, I never would have survived these past three years. Without the people that rallied around Janet, loving and honoring her, she would not have made the amazing recovery she has.

Since her injury, Janet survived her coma and is now living at home. She went from being in a wheelchair to walking unassisted for half a kilometer. She progressed from speaking one or two words in a whisper to sharing her story in front of a university class and on live radio. From being fed through a tube, to creating and helping prepare her own meals. Throughout this surreal and challenging journey, God brought the right people into Janet's and my life. Each of them honored Janet by loving her and helping her in different ways. Some sang to her, read stories, some worked with colors, and some just sat and prayed. She received love and opportunities that few people receive. Romans 12:10 speaks not only to couples, but how we show respect and love to everyone in our circle of influence. "Team Save Janet" proved that when we honor one another in this way, blessings and rewards are beyond anything we can imagine.[64]

I watched as Larry lovingly but firmly attended to Janet's every need. He put his career on hold to be by her side every day to encourage and motivate her throughout the rehabilitation process. He sold their existing home and had a new house renovated for wheelchair access, and he painted the walls Janet's favorite color, yellow. He honored her, was committed to her, and made sacrifices we rarely see in marriages.

Imagine if we all took the "honor one another" principle as seriously as Larry and Janet did. Not only would we live a life of no regrets, but we'd also receive rewards and blessings from our Heavenly Father in ways that would fulfill and enrich our lives to overflowing. Because God promises that he has rewards for us.

REWARDS

Honor carries with it great rewards. God wants to promote us, make our lives easier, and give us certain advantages. I know he has our best interests at heart and is working everything for our good. God wants us to do our part so that he can do his part. Once we are aware of this concept, we will begin to see God's blessings and rewards in the ordinary details of life. Here are some verses that affirm this:

True humility and respect for the Lord lead a man
to riches, honor, and long life.
Proverbs 22:4 TLB

In everything you do, put God first, and
he will direct you and crown your efforts with success.
Proverbs 3:6 TLB

So when your faith remains strong through many trials,
it will bring you much praise and glory and honor on the day
when Jesus Christ is revealed to the whole world.
1 Peter 1:7 NLT

I believe that because I've honored my parents, God is rewarding me with honor from my children and grandchildren. My children
observed how I talked to my mother and watched me sacrifice my
personal agenda to attend to her needs until her death. My family saw
how I honored my father during the difficult days of his struggle with
ALS. Now I reap the blessings and rewards of having my children
shower me with respect and love. God has rewarded me with health
and financial blessings in ways I could never have dreamed or imagined. I truly feel he has placed a crown of honor on my head, and this
is available to every one of us.

FULFILL YOUR SOUL

We can expect honor and glory not because of what we do or who
we are, but because of whom we belong to—our Heavenly Father. I
know from personal experience that when we live "heavenly minded,"
honoring God and declaring his goodness in our lives, we will stand
amazed at how he wants to bless and reward us.

1. One of the most powerful ways you can honor God in everything
   you do is starting your day with prayer. Genuine prayer changes
   hearts. Every day before you leave the house, pray and declare
   God's favor in your life. Then take the time to look around, ex-
   pecting doors to open in simple yet astonishing ways.
2. Never take God's favor for granted. Every day, tell him, "Thank
   you for helping me. Thank you for giving me everything I need."

When you pray with thankfulness, you will remember how many blessings you have already.

3. Read Psalm 23 and remind yourself of the powerful affirmation of how God wants to pour his love and favor onto your life. "Because the Lord is my Shepherd, I have everything I need. He helps me do what honors him the most. You provide delicious food for me in the presence of my enemies. Your goodness and unfailing kindness shall be with me all of my life."

4. We love the feeling of receiving honor. Remember that your children and grandchildren are watching how you honor your parents. You'll experience fulfillment beyond measure when your children honor and respect you.

5. Rewards await you. The law of reaping and sowing always comes back to you. "See to it that you win your full reward from the Lord" (2 John 1:8 TLB). If you are loyal and obedient to Christ's teachings, you will receive your full reward of blessings and honor. To receive a full reward, you need to exercise this in every aspect of your life: your workplaces, home, neighborhood, grocery store, church and even the golf course.

6. Honor is a heart issue. True honor is extended without hypocrisy or ulterior motives for some kind of gain. God promises rewards if you pursue his honor and godliness. It may not come immediately or when you think it should, but it always comes.

S.T.O.P. AND ASK GOD TO HELP YOU
FULFILL YOUR SOUL

BEGIN BY ASKING: *How do I honor people who don't deserve it?*

S-Scripture: "Your own soul is nourished when you are kind; it is destroyed when you are cruel" (Proverbs 11:17 TLB).

T-Thanksgiving: "Thank you for being a good and fair God. Thank you for rewarding me and nourishing my soul when I'm obedient to honor all the people you place in my life."

O-Observation: Through my human eyes there are many people who don't deserve honor. People who are cruel, who lie, cheat, steal, and commit murders. I have to remember this Scripture: "Yes each of us will give an account of himself to God" (Romans 14:12 TLB). I must do my part in treating everyone with respect—and leave the judgment up to God.

P-Prayer: "God, please forgive me for criticizing or neglecting to honor those you have placed in my life. Forgive me when I feel justified in being unkind, and when I don't submit to your authority and treat everyone as one of your valuable children. Immerse my heart and soul with true honor, so that I can treat everyone with loving motives. Help me to set healthy boundaries when others' expectations and actions are ungodly. Teach me how to show respect to all people in authority. Thank you for helping me. Amen."

CHAPTER 9

FULFILLMENT THROUGH BLESSING ONE ANOTHER

Prosperity on My Knees

When you focus on being a blessing,
God makes sure that you are always blessed in abundance.
—JOEL OSTEEN

I CONFESS, MOST OF MY LIFE I casually threw the words "bless you" around as a good luck charm, hoping to brighten someone's day. I never expected to find that blessings have hauntingly beautiful power to enrich our lives with joy and fulfillment.

It started when I signed a contract to write devotionals for Scripture Union Canada for a new online Bible application called "The Story." Assigned Genesis 27 through Genesis 48, I immediately caught the essence of the chapters as they unfolded like a Steven Spielberg movie. Now my challenge was to discover and apply biblical truths and principles.

I became fully engrossed in this family drama when the mother in the story, Rebekah, helped her favorite son and "mamma's boy," Jacob, steal the blessing from his older brother, Esau. Only a restless soul, longing for greed and power would be compelled to orchestrate something so evil. Obviously, they knew something about blessings that I did not.

The story unfolds as Esau comes back from his hunting expedition to find that while he was gone, his brother, Jacob, had pretended to be him and deceived their father into giving Jacob the blessing. Esau became furious, but also heartbroken. It wrecks me when I read his response for this treacherous deceit. "But don't you have just one blessing for me, Father? Oh bless me my father! Bless me!' Esau sobbed inconsolably" (Genesis 27:38 MSG). Esau knew that his father held a blessing in his hand, which was the key to prosperity for his future and that of his children. Like Esau, down through the ages many children have sought the blessings of their earthly fathers. With the knowledge of this deep longing, I felt inspired to begin an intense study on blessings.

WHAT DOES BLESSING MEAN?

The first time the word *blessed* appears in Scripture is in the creation story, when on the fifth day, God created the birds, fish, and all sea creatures. "And God looked at them with pleasure and blessed them all" (Genesis 1:22 TLB). The Hebrew word for create is *bara*, and the word for blessed is *barak*.[65] After researching further, I began to see the relationship of these two words and how the manifestation of a blessing is actually creation at work. A blessing unleashes creative ability for the words to bear fruit.

> *A blessing unleashes creative ability*
> *for the words to bear fruit.*

When we impart God's word of blessing, we empower them to grow, flourish, and prosper in every area of their lives. I agree with what Joseph Cavanaugh III wrote in his book, *Language of Blessing*. "Blessings are prophetic in that they communicate the heart, mind, and will of God for an individual. They connect us with our Creator's dream for us. Words of blessing affirm and empower God-given intrinsic attributes, such as personality, gifting, talents, character traits, and intelligences." Cavanaugh goes on to say, "Your words bring forth life or death. That may sound melodramatic or overstated; I assure you it is not. What you say has the power to give life to dreams and callings or to snuff them out before they have a chance to develop"[66]

I could hardly grasp the enormity of that concept. You and I can literally impart God's image deep into the heart of a person, by helping them understand who they are and their purpose on this earth.

IMPARTING BLESSINGS

I didn't know anything about imparting blessings to my children when they were growing up. It made me sad and distraught to think that I missed out on giving them something so meaningful and powerful. An excerpt in Jack Hayford's book *Blessing Your Children*[67] assured me it is never too late. He writes, "God has given parents the privilege and power to speak blessing upon their children and with that blessing to advance life, health, growth, joy, and self-confidence. We need to learn to steward this privilege as a dynamic aspect of raising our children and blessing them in every way we possibly can."

In light of that reassurance, I came up with a great plan.

In the midst of my research on blessings, Jack and I were knee-deep into planning our upcoming family reunion. One summer evening on our deck, as we pored over creative ideas, I came up with something. "What would you think about having a 'Blessing Evening'? I'm not quite sure what it will look like, but let's start by writing out a blessing for each grandchild and reading this blessing over them during a beautifully-designed evening." Jack caught my excitement, and we began to outline what a blessing would look like. After some research, we concluded that there was no real right or wrong way to write a blessing, so we created our own design. We began by researching the meaning of each grandchild's name. We learned that the name Mya means "great one," Austin means "great and magnificent," and Alex means "protector of men/man's defender." Once we had the biblical meanings for all nine grandchildren, we used their names as the springboard to help us unpack how their names were already defining their present characteristics and abilities. Next, we listed their natural talents and accomplishments, and segued that into how we imagined God using those gifts for their future. Finally, we picked a suitable Bible verse and ended the blessing with a prayer. Here is one example, for our little Mya, who was four years old at the time:

It is said that the name Mya means "great one." You have already shown your family and friends what great things you can do. We know you love to dance, and you do it so well. We have seen your legs flying down the soccer field, jumping, and rolling in gymnastics and on your trampoline, swimming like a fish, and skiing down a huge mountain. You have already completed preschool in two different schools, you can write your own name, and you have so many friends.

You are one of God's great little girls. He sent you down from Heaven just at the right time to bring joy into this family. God has great plans for you Mya. He has given you beauty, a radiant smile, a loving heart, a creative mind, and a tender but bold and courageous spirit. God has wrapped many wonderful things up in a great package called Mya.

There is nothing more beautiful than a girl who knows she is loved. Mya, you are loved! God has blessed you with a family that loves and adores you. May God's love always strengthen you and give you courage. God has great plans for you. Let him help you discover all life has for you on this earth. Do not be afraid! Even in your young years, may you learn to trust God in such a way that you know that nothing in this world can stop you from fulfilling the purposes God has called you to. You are great . . . and greatly loved. We bless you in the name of Jesus.

> For I can do everything with the help of Christ
> who gives me the strength I need.
> Philippians 4:13 NLT

The Blessing Evening unfolded on a magical summer night on the deck of our home. We surrounded ourselves with family and only a few close friends, hoping for an intimate, vulnerable, powerful event. As Jack and I called up each grandchild, read their blessing, and prayed for them, the atmosphere was shrouded in a deep sense of love and belonging that I can only describe as soaking in the presence of the Holy Spirit.

A sweet hush lingered over our deck as we wiped away tears and deeply hoped God would bear fruit and accomplish all the words spoken over each child. My spirit felt a great sense of longing, and I wondered if perhaps I wasn't the only adult present who wished they had received that kind of blessing from our fathers or mothers. I thought about how Esau had cried out to his dad, "Oh my father, bless me too!" (Genesis 27:38 NLT).

OBSTACLES TO BLESSINGS

When I saw how the Blessing Evening impacted us, I realized we all desire for someone to speak goodness into our lives. We are put on this earth to do this for each other so we can all prosper, while using all the gifts and abilities God has poured into us. The Bible reminds us that God has already blessed us with everything we need. "How we praise God, the Father of our Lord Jesus Christ, who has blessed us with every blessing in heaven because we belong to Christ" (Ephesians 1:3 TLB). But it doesn't end there. God has blessed us, so we can now pour that blessing onto one another. I felt blessed and fulfilled pondering on, praying for, and preparing the blessings for my grandchildren. Now I better understand this Scripture: "The one who blesses others is abundantly blessed; those who help others are helped" (Proverbs 11:25 MSG).

But we have to first overcome a few grievous problems.

1. Most of us don't understand the impact of blessings. When someone sneezes, we quickly respond with a vague "God bless you." We sign our e-mails and greeting cards with "Blessings," and it sounds very Christian and friendly. Without an understanding of the full power and potential of this age-old cliché, we throw it around like a meaningless penny.
2. Most of us never received a blessing from our parents, and we want a blessing for ourselves. We're not ready to pour blessings on others and enrich their lives, when we desire our own lives to flourish.
3. We don't feel worthy to receive a blessing from God or another human being. We have too many feelings of guilt, shame, and

worthlessness to internalize how much God wants to bless everyone. His blessing is always available to us; we have to choose to
receive it.

4. Our restless spirits want more, just for us. We're too greedy to
   give it away.
5. We don't know how.

God made a promise to Abram (who later became Abraham). "I will
bless you and make your name famous, and you will be a blessing to
many others. I will bless those who bless you and curse those who curse
you; and the entire world will be blessed because of you" (Genesis 12:3
NLT). Yes, that blessing was meant for Abraham, but God never gives
up on his original plan or goes back on his promises. God passed the
blessing from Abraham to Jesus, and from Jesus to us. "He redeemed us
in order that the blessing given to Abraham might come to the Gentiles
through Christ Jesus" (Galatians 3:14 NIV).

BLESSINGS OR CURSES

Unfortunately, these same mouths that can spout beautiful, enriching blessings can also speak evil, causing harm and destroying
lives. The Bible warns about this. "With our tongues we bless God
our Father, with the same tongues we curse the very men and women
he made in his image. Curses and blessings out of the same mouth"
(James 3:9–10 MSG).

Let's be honest. We don't believe everyone deserves to be blessed.
We may look down on people who have messed up their lives. The
ragged, dirty teenager peddling for money at the side of the street. The
person who has murdered. Or the neighbor who was caught in a drug
ring. We may even go so far as to curse the one who embezzles from a
company, ruining lives, or the one who wrecks their wonderful family
life by having an affair. A curse is "an expressed wish that some form
of adversity or misfortune will befall or attach to some other entity—
one or more persons."[68] Often, it's more natural to curse someone than
speak a blessing over his or her life. But we have to realize that the

same power that causes our lives to flourish can, by cursing, cause lives to be destroyed. We must be deliberate about the words we use when we speak to or about other people.

"Today I have given you the choice between life and death, between blessings and curses. Now I call on heaven and earth to witness the choice you make" (Deuteronomy 30:19 NLT).

Our words hold power. With our words, we can help "one another" flourish and unleash the satisfying lives we were designed to enjoy, or we can diminish the person's confidence, self-esteem, and value. In the heat of a moment, when our emotions rage with injustice or anger, we must stop and consider the consequences of blessings versus curses.

In my experience, I have found that speaking words of blessing over someone's life can actually break the power of a curse. A number of years ago, a person spoke harsh and cruel words that left me feeling shredded and angry. Those words seemed like a curse because I felt diminished as a human being, and I believe the person who spoke them wanted adversity and misfortune to fall my way. I first reacted with thoughts of retaliating with hurtful words. But I made myself stop, rethink, and reload my heart with the consequences of my actions. As I drove home that evening, I recalled the power of speaking words of blessing. Even though that person was not in the car with me, I spoke words of blessing out loud, as though he were beside me. I blessed his career, his family, his mind, and his success for every endeavor in his life. By the time I walked through the back door of my home, those words of blessing had in fact healed my incensed spirit, and I felt kinder and more compassionate toward him.

Blessings and curses are supernatural transactions, and only God knows the impact they have on our hearts. But I know that my spoken blessings broke the anger and harsh words lodged in my heart and stopped me from retaliating with ugly actions. I felt peaceful and grateful that God used my obedience to change my heart rather than cause more harm. It's hard to accomplish, but I now have my own clear evidence that choosing words of blessing encourages our hearts to keep beating with love.

WE ALL DESERVE A BLESSING

By the time I finished writing my devotionals for Scripture Union, I was fully aware of the power of blessings on Jacob's life. Jacob endured many hardships but also blessings in his life, as many of us do. Commentaries tend to suggest, and I agree, that Jacob never fully forgot his deceitful act of stealing his brother Esau's blessing. This is illustrated so powerfully when, in his old age, he is asked by his beloved son Joseph to bless his two sons, Ephraim and Manasseh. According to custom, the father (or grandfather) would place his right hand on the oldest child, who was the one entitled to receive a blessing.

Here is how the story reads in Genesis:

> Joseph took the boys by the hand, bowed deeply to him, and led the boys to their grandfather's knees—Ephraim at Israel's left hand and Manasseh at his right. But Israel crossed his arms as he stretched them out to lay his hands upon the boys' heads, so that his right hand was upon the head of Ephraim, the younger boy, and his left hand upon the head of Manasseh the older. He did this purposely . . . But Joseph was upset and displeased when he saw that his father had laid his right hand on Ephraim's head; so he lifted it to place it on Manasseh's head instead. "No, father," he said, "You've got your right hand on the wrong head! This one over here is the older. Put your right hand on him!" But his father refused. "I know what I'm doing my son," he said. "Manasseh too shall become a great nation, but his younger brother shall become even greater" (Genesis 48:12–19 TLB).

This dialogue at the end of Jacob (Israel's) life impacted me profoundly. I agree with the commentaries[69] stating that Jacob wanted to redeem a wrong he had purposefully committed when he was a young lad. He stole a blessing that he did not deserve, and yet, because of God's grace, he had received the fruit of the blessing. So he crossed his arms and blessed the son who did not rightfully deserve the blessing.

We see the unfairness when blessings fall on both the just and unjust. But Jesus came to die for all of us, and in his marvelous grace he wants to shower blessings on our lives. "Blessed be God, the Father of our Lord Jesus the Anointed One, who grants us every spiritual blessing in these heavenly realms *where we live* in the Anointed—*not because of anything we have done, but because of what He has done for us*" (Ephesians 1:3 VOICE).

God has placed us on this earth to bless each other, and perhaps especially to bless those around us who feel they don't deserve it.

BLESS ONE ANOTHER

Imagine what our world would be like if we blessed our children as they began to explore who they are and why they exist. Jesus values children. In the book of Mark, we read how people brought their little children to Jesus so he could touch them. But Jesus' disciples shooed them off. When Jesus saw this, he was irate and rebuked them with these words: "'Don't push these children away. Don't ever get between them and me. These children are at the very center of life in the kingdom' . . . Then gathering the children up in his arms, he laid his hands of blessing on them" (Mark 10:14–19 MSG).

The Jewish custom for blessing children still exists today. On Friday nights, some Jewish families perform a short ritual before they sit down to dinner. A personal, tender moment in which the parent (usually the father) places his hand upon their heads, one after another, and says a blessing over each child. I can't imagine what it would feel like to have someone speak words of love and affirmation over me every Friday. I can surely understand how a recipient of such love would feel confident, find fulfillment, and thrive in this complicated world. Children thirst for parental acceptance and approval, and they need others to reinforce their worth. It's never too late.

When I babysit my grandchildren or when they come to visit, I look for every opportunity to affirm their gifts and unleash their abilities. Several of our grandchildren are now teenagers or young adults, and every once in a while I text them to let them know I'm thinking about them and praying for them. When my grandson Matthew was little, each night as I tucked him into bed, I prayed with him and made up a song about all the good things God and I love about him. He's too old now, but I pray he will always remember those words of love and affirmation.

Here are other practical ways we can bless our children every day:

- A whisper of love in their ear, giving them quiet assurance that you will pray for them during an exam or sport competition.
- A simple pat on the back.
- When they get bigger, an arm around the shoulder and a squeeze to let them know they are special to you.
- A word to diffuse some disappointment or rejection.
- Tucking them into bed with a song and prayer.
- For older ones, a text message or affirming them in a Facebook post.
- Listening to them without judgment.
- Telling them you understand.

But let's not forget our grown-up hearts are still vulnerable and need others to speak words of affirmation into our spirits. In the midst of my research, I asked God to help me write a blessing I could share with the women I speak to at conferences. One day, sitting at my computer, God inspired me with these words:

> God designed and prepared you for a time such as this,
> For a glorious life, filled with purpose and bliss.
>
> May the wind of the Spirit refresh you with wisdom,
> As you lay down your life for his glorious Kingdom.
>
> Nothing you do for him is neglected or lost,
> Yes, your time is precious and at a very high cost.
>
> But remember each day Jesus bought you for a price,
> It's not just good luck, or a winning roll of the dice.
> Your failures and mistakes are all covered with love,

By drops of blood poured down from a cross up above.

He did this for you; his radical redemption set you free,
To be the masterpiece that he designed you to be.

You are a creation so beautiful as unique as a star.
God knows your name; he is always near and not far.

He is your rescuer, supporter, and advocate, too,
His arms are wide open when you're feeling lost and blue.

"Yes," he said, "In this world there will be trouble."
But he left you his Spirit to help sort through your rubble.

But remember to pray, so that Heaven can open wide,
To know that in your trouble God is always at your side.

So gird up your soul and laugh in the face of fear,
There is nothing too huge when you know God is near.

In your insecurity and weakness, you know he is strong,
So reach for his hand; that is where you belong.

This radical love, so mysterious and free,
Can open your heart and help you to see.

That each tear that falls is a seed to grow beauty,
God will comfort and embrace you not out of duty.

But because you are his child and he is shaping you for Glory.
So that he can write his name at the end of your story.

At the end of all my conferences, I make it a practice to have the women stand up in groups of two or three, facing each other. I have them repeat a blessing to each other, words pertinent to the content of the weekend. Tears always flow. I think we all are crying deep in our hearts to hear words that let us know we are enough, and we're acceptable the way God made us. When I see how God's words stir their hearts, it fills me to overflowing.

FULFILL YOUR SOUL

The strange thing about blessing others is that, in return, we also feel blessed and fulfilled. I wrote this chapter while fully immersed in preparations for a wedding shower for my dear friend Joanne, who, at the age of fifty-three, is marrying the love of her life. Instead of the usual wedding shower, where people bring vases and bowls they don't need, two of her close friends and I prepared an evening of blessings. We asked all the attendees to e-mail us their pictures and words of blessing. Then we incorporated all those beautiful pictures and meaningful words into a colorful and inspirational book and presented it to her at this unique and special event.

Amazingly, it was the three of us who prepared for this distinctive shower that felt thoroughly blessed. As women read their blessings to Joanne, our hearts were fulfilled with the satisfaction that comes from pouring something beautiful into another person's life.

---

*The strange thing about blessing others is
that, in return, we also feel blessed and fulfilled.*

I have seen and experienced the power of blessings, and I encourage you to let it become a natural and beautiful habit in your life. Blessings can come in the form of words, actions, or even tangible goods that will enhance and empower a person's life.

Try these seven ways to satisfy your soul:

1. Hang around with people who see the best in you. "Blessed is the one who does not walk in step with the wicked or stand

in the way that sinners take or sit in the company of mockers" (Psalm 1:1 NIV).

2. Each morning, before I start my day, I ask God to place someone in my life I can bless. Try this for one month and see how it blesses you.

3. Instead of buying the next birthday or Christmas card for your husband, sister, or friend, write out a blessing and speak it aloud to them.

4. The next time someone offends you or makes you angry, stop, breathe, and deliberately say a blessing over them. Say it quietly to yourself or to them—whatever is appropriate at the time.

5. Make the word *blessing* your word for the upcoming year, and ask God to teach you what it means to be a blessing to others.

6. Give away something valuable. "Don't hoard your goods; spread them around. Be a blessing to others" (Ecclesiastes 11:2 MSG).

7. Share your faith with others so they too can experience God's blessings. "As you share your faith with others, I pray that they may come to know all the blessings Christ has given us" (Philemon 1:6 CEV).

S.T.O.P. AND ASK GOD TO HELP YOU
FULFILL YOUR SOUL

BEGIN BY ASKING: *Who can I bless today?*

S-Scripture: "The one who blesses others is abundantly blessed; those who help others are helped" (Proverbs 11:25 MSG).

T-Thanksgiving: "It amazes me that in spite of my flaws and failures, you still want to bless me. Thank you that goodness is available to me each day and that you want to pour good things into my life to help me be fulfilled."

O-Observation: It is hard me for me to grasp the counterintuitive concept that if I bless others I will in turn be blessed and fulfilled. I must make a deliberate choice to learn more about the power of blessings, so I can freely and joyfully make it a daily habit in my life.

P-Prayer: "God, I confess that I seek blessings for my own life, and I don't often think about the concept of blessing others. Help me learn more about the power of blessings, so I can apply this significant principle in the lives of people I encounter each day. Especially, help me take note of little children, so I can stop and pour your love and affirmation into their little spirits. Help me become a "blesser of people" so my actions make this world a better place, while in turn my soul is satisfied and joyful. Amen."

CHAPTER 10

FULFILLMENT THROUGH PRAYING FOR ONE ANOTHER

The Boulder in My Pathway

Prayer is not a check request asking for things from God.
It is a deposit slip—a way of depositing God's character
into our bankrupt souls.
—DUTCH SHEETS

OUR FRIENDSHIP BLOSSOMED through prayer. It ignited when three of us attended the Advanced Writer and Speaker's Conference in Atlanta, Georgia and huddled in a prayer circle experiencing the sweetness of God's presence. When the prayer time was over, we looked up, smiled, and reluctantly pushed our seats back into position to continue with the conference session. Something felt unfinished. Sure enough, Sheryl seized the moment and bravely expressed the lingering desire in all our hearts.

"This prayer time was so amazing," she said. "When this conference is over, I would love to pray with both of you at least once a month." Saundra and I eagerly nodded in agreement, but there was one small hitch. All three of us live in different parts of North America. Saundra is a physician, author, and speaker living in Anniston, Alabama. Sheryl resides in Bakersfield, California, and she's also an author, speaker, and radio personality. Of course, I live in Kelowna, Canada. How was this going to work?

We brainstormed and came up with a workable plan. Each month we would set a date, send each other praise items and prayer requests, then pray for each other for an hour or so on a Skype conference call. All three of us are passionate about praying for one another, like the Bible recommends. "Admit your faults to one another and pray for each other so that you may be healed. The earnest prayer of a righteous person has great power and wonderful results" (James 5:16 TLB). The three of us agreed we are in desperate need of prayer for God to help us navigate life, trusting him completely to help us find and prepare speaking engagements and publishers for our books. We know we must be intentional about setting time aside to take our insurmountable requests and problems into the presence of the King of the universe, the creator of Heaven and Earth. He is our Father, who already knows our story from beginning to end and is interested in every detail of our lives.

In *Too Busy Not to Pray,* Bill Hybels says,

> Awareness of God's presence comes as a result of taking time to speak and listen to him through prayer; conversely, the power of prayer is unleashed in the lives of those who spend time in God's presence.[70]

He goes on to say,

> God is interested in your prayers because he is interested in you. Whatever matters to you is a priority for his attention. Nothing in the universe matters as much to him as what is going on in your life this day. You don't have to pester him to get his attention. You don't necessarily have to spend hours on your knees or flail yourself or go without food to show him that you really mean business. He's your Father and he wants to hear what you have to say.[71]

Since August 2014, Saundra, Sheryl, and I scheduled time each month to pray for one another—our children, husbands, ministries, and the endless hurdles and challenges that show up in our pathways. Once we see each other's faces on the Skype screen, the physical distance seems to vanish. Our hearts become connected through our like-minded need for prayer as we share our deepest longings, challenges, and hindrances. Throughout the next hour, we lay all concerns at the foot of the cross, and become empowered to enjoy victory beyond our current struggles.

THE BOULDERS

We all have hopes, dreams, and longings in our hearts that life will unfold a certain way. But at any time along this beautiful and successful journey, a huge obstacle can suddenly show up in our pathway. A seemingly insurmountable obstruction we can't get around or push out of the way. These uninvited hindrances can come in the form of:

- Bankruptcy.
- Your spouse blurting out, "I don't love you anymore, and I am moving out."
- A sudden, tragic death. The day Sheryl's husband was killed on his motorcycle.
- Hearing the doctor say, "You are infertile and will never be able to have a baby."
- Hearing, "You're fired."
- Discovering your spouse is addicted to pornography.
- Finding out your child has been diagnosed with a mental illness.

You may initially react with shock, disbelief, and anger. Then a gut-wrenching bitterness may grow inside you toward this unwanted complication and heartache. You may become overwhelmed, lying awake night after night, wondering why God would allow this boulder in your path. Some shake their fists in anger and turn away from God. Others turn to alcohol, drugs, food, or another relationship to dull the searing pain. But I'm astounded how painful obstacles have actually empowered my own prayer life, giving me hope beyond anything I could ever imagine. Now I comprehend this verse: "Careful! I've put a huge stone on the road to Mount Zion, a stone you can't get around. But the stone is me! If you're looking for me, you'll find me on the way, not in the way" (Romans 9:12 MSG).

Let that sink in for a moment. The stone is Jesus. He is not *in* the way. He is *the* way. That stone is a boulder disguised as the love and mercy of Jesus to strengthen, fulfill, and make us wiser than we could ever dream.

It's hard enough for us to overcome a painful obstruction in our own journey. But it's even harder when it shows up in our children's pathways.

The stone is Jesus. He is not in the way. He is the way.

When my son Donovan was seventeen, I watched him turn away from God, question our family values, and become disinterested in church. He had his own version of hopes and dreams and his plan was unfolding beautifully. Eventually, he had his PhD in rhetoric, a lovely Texan wife, a teaching job at the University of Las Vegas, and a new home. Then a boulder showed up. The economy crashed, he lost this home, and his marriage fell apart. Because of the impending divorce, he was unable to complete the application for his green card, and he had to move back to Canada for an entire year. Two weeks before Christmas 2010, his Range Rover showed up in our driveway with his personal belongings stacked to the roof. He moved back home with us for the next year. He was stuck behind a boulder so huge it seemed insurmountable.

At seventeen, I also turned away from God, the church, and our family's values. I was determined to do life my way. During my rebellious teenage years, I often missed my curfew and quietly snuck past my parent's bedroom. Once, something made me stop and listen. It was the beautiful, rhythmic sound of my mother praying. That memory lingers in my heart, empowering me to believe Jesus' promise: "Ask, using my name, and you will receive, and your cup of joy will overflow" (John 16:24 TLB).

While Donovan and our family were behind that enormous

boulder, I knew one day we would again experience tremendous joy. My experience tells me that it's when we're stuck behind obstacles that we're likely to make life-changing choices.

BEHIND THE BOULDER

Behind the boulder, we are raw and vulnerable. We feel ripped away from everything that provided our security, comfort, or even love. When our hopes and dreams are dashed, we ask hard, introspective questions.

> *Have I done something wrong?*
> *Is God withholding his love?*
> *Why is this happening to me?*
> *Will I ever be happy again?*

We go through myriad tumultuous feelings; rejection, fear, sadness, disappointment. Often, depression follows right on the heels of despair. I believe the greatest strategy Satan uses is making people feel God has placed the huge rock there to sabotage our hopes and crush our spirits. Satan wants to deceive us into becoming angry and, ultimately, turning away from God. The enemy knows that without God and hope, we perish.

The Land Between

I call this desolate and lonely place behind the boulder "the land between." It is that desert place where Moses and the Israelites wandered for forty year, learning to trust God for daily provision and guidance. Let's redefine our thinking to see this barren place as God's greatest plan for our formation.

- He wants to accomplish things in us that can't be accomplished any other way.
- He knows things about the future we don't.
- Discoveries are made in this place, and lessons are learned.
- We are challenged to ask, "Do I really trust God?"

Sometimes the land between is the result and consequence of our own sin and bad choices. But God is always with us. Let's not forget that God was with the Israelites as a cloud during the day and fire at night for their entire desert sojourn. Even while they complained, whined, and grumbled, God provided water and food, and their shoes never wore out. God continues to love us and remind us that he is always with us. Especially in the land between.

> In my distress I screamed to the Lord for his help.
> And he heard me from heaven; my cry reached his ears.
> Psalm 18:6 TLB

> He does not ignore the prayers of men in trouble
> when they call to him for help.
> Psalm 8:12 TLB

> For I cried to him and he answered me!
> He freed me from all my fears.
> Psalm 34:4 TLB

> The Lord is close to those whose hearts are breaking;
> he rescues those who are humbly sorry for their sins.
> Psalm 34:18 TLB

I followed in my mother's footsteps in praying for my children. From the time Donovan turned away from God as a teenager, I prayed for him almost daily. I prayed he would renew his personal relationship with God and turn to God for an outpouring of love, peace, and grace. Throughout the year Donovan lived with us, he regularly attended church and frequently asked insightful and perplexing spiritual questions. Donovan and I loved spending time together in the kitchen, and we sat at the counter for hours discussing the Bible and God. Those were enriching times of deep and engaging conversations, laughter, and renewed hope. Our "kitchen conversations" ended abruptly when Donovan contracted to teach in Beijing, China for five months. I hoped our rich dialogue had softened his heart to seek God for wisdom and guidance as he pursued this new and challenging adventure. But by the time I put him on the plane he had not made any commitment to dedicate his life to God. I was heartbroken, but quickly recovered after making a bold decision. I promised the Lord I would pray for Donovan until I took my last breath, and I would leave the results up to God. I declared that Donovan is God's child, and that God has a good plan for his future.

> While we are in this barren, desert place without any results, we need to be reminded of Mark Batterson's words in *The Circle Maker*: "God is not holding out or holding back. It's not in His nature to withhold any good thing from us. He most certainly won't bless disobedience, but He most certainly will bless obedience. If you take God at His word, you'll make the joyful discovery that God wants to bless you far more than you want to be blessed. And His capacity to give is far greater than your capacity to receive."[72]

I looked up Psalm 84:11 and was reassured that our God is a good God. "No good thing will he withhold from those who walk his paths." I needed to be obedient to do my part—love and pray.

The War Room

Being raw and vulnerable leaves us open for Satan to discourage and leave us feeling defeated. Like the Israelites wandering endlessly in the desert, we lose perspective and just want the comfort and security of the old life. The people of Israel forgot that God set them free from their slavery of torture and hardship. Yet, they whined and complained: "Oh, that we had some of the delicious fish we enjoyed so much in Egypt, and the wonderful cucumbers and melons, leeks, onions, and garlic!" (Numbers 11:4–5 TLB). When we are hurting and feel alone, our minds deceive us and we want anything to make us feel better. But we need to be aware, Satan wants to keep us locked in our defeat because his purpose is to "steal, kill, and destroy" (John 10:10 TLB). Many of our battlefields are in our mind. The apostle Paul reminds us of this: "For our struggle is not against flesh and blood, but against the rulers, against the authorities, against the powers of this dark world and against the spiritual forces of evil in the heavenly realms" (Ephesians 6:12 NIV). The only way to win this supernatural battle is through supernatural power—on our knees.

We begin moving forward from a stance of victory. After Donovan left for Beijing, I took on this powerful posture, faithfully praying and leaving the results to God.

We begin moving forward from a stance of victory.

My friend Saundra also believes that prayer is the power that gives us the strength and courage to move beyond the boulder. This is her story of how she took a stance and encouraged her medical office to go to war.

Spring has always been my favorite season, yet this spring did not bring the fresh beauty of new life. It brought death, after death, after death.

This particular day started out as every other day when I showed up to work. An hour into seeing patients in my medical office, everything changed. My nurse was in hysterics after receiving a phone call that her husband had not yet arrived at his workplace. "He leaves for work at 5 a.m.," she said. "And now it's 9:30 a.m. He's not answering his cell phone, and I know it hasn't gone dead because not keeping phones charged is one of his pet peeves."

Twenty minutes later, a police officer walked into the clinic and stood at the entrance to my nurse's office. He told her, "Your husband has been killed in a fatal collision." Her scream was heard throughout the two stories of the medical complex. I will never forget that sound. The raw agony of it pierced something in my soul.

My nurse was screaming, "No, God, no!" The ten patients in the waiting room had heard the officer deliver the tragic news, and many sat silently and wept into their hands. Doctors and staff from all over the building came running at the sound of her screams. It was an emotional war zone. It was as if that officer walked in and dropped a bomb.

This tragedy was the first of a stream of events. A month after the death of my nurse's husband, our nurse practitioner's brother-in-law was killed in a car accident. A month after that, my fifteen-year-old nephew was hit by a truck in front of his home while riding his bike. He died in transit to the Emergency Room. A few months later, another nurse lost her husband in a tragic car accident. Three young fathers, leaving six children ranging in ages from three to eleven. Parents grieving the loss of their son every time they drive past the spot where he died on the road in front of their home. These events left the staff numb as we went from one funeral to another.

Relationships and love were the power that kept us connected, but grief led us to the idea for a prayer room. We called it our war room, the place where we could war with the pain and sorrow and move into a place of victory. In contrast to the impersonal nature of clinical exam rooms, this room was dedicated to the presence of God. As staff entered, their tears expressed their pain, speaking words their hearts were unable to utter. Corkboards held pinned prayer requests. Names were called out before the throne of God on behalf of a co-worker in need of his comfort, his peace, and his joy. Instead of our circumstances causing us to become bitter, they lead us to pray for one another. Those prayers brought with them the healing and victory we all desperately needed.[73]

Many of us have tragic stories. Marriages fall apart, leaving debris and endless heartache. Children and parents are left to deal with anxiety and trauma. Jack and I watched the movie *The War Room[74]* and were so encouraged that a film producer saw the value of prayer to help with misunderstanding and strife in marriages.

God gave us the supernatural weapon of prayer, and told us to use it. "Pray all the time. Ask God for anything in line with the Holy Spirit's wishes. Plead with him, reminding him of your needs, and keep praying earnestly for all Christians everywhere" (Ephesians 6:18 TLB). Saundra's poignant story beautifully describes the power of prayer. Prayer doesn't necessarily fix circumstances, but it enables God to heal our broken hearts, to give us fresh hope, and to overcome the boulder.

BEYOND THE BOULDER

One day we will come out of our desert-wandering and enjoy sweet victory on the other side of that huge obstruction. One small word determines the outcome. Read this verse and see if you can find the one word. "For I know the plans I have for you, says the Lord. They are plans for good and not for evil, to give you a future and a hope. In those days when you pray, I will listen. You will find me when you seek me, if you look for me in earnest" (Jeremiah 29:11-13 TLB).

The small word is "if." *If* we choose to seek God, on our knees, pleading for help to conquer our boulders, we will be victorious. Our prayers may never change our circumstances, but they will change our hearts. They'll also change our thinking and perspective, and we'll find new freedom and joy in ways we could never predict or orchestrate on our own.

Our prayers may never change our circumstances, but they will change our hearts.

Three weeks after Donovan arrived in Beijing, he sent us an e-mail. It was almost midnight when I saw it land in my inbox. Even though I was tired, my curious mind wanted to read about his latest adventures in China. I shouted for Jack to come read it with me. Together, we read the words I thought we might never hear. Donovan explained how, while sitting in a Starbucks in one of the most populated countries on the planet, he'd had a God-encounter. After years and years of wandering, he wanted to embrace God's love and take first steps into the unknown with God at his side. He said God's love poured over him with such power he had to pull his sweater over his head for fear of scaring the other patrons.

When he came back from Beijing, he lived differently. He had to make many difficult choices, allowing God to help him rebuild his life from ground up. He became involved in his city, volunteering in a community garden and being a big brother to a younger boy. He is again teaching at the University of Las Vegas, and making choices that are kinder, wiser, and more fulfilling. That's what happens when we invite God to help us get unstuck—out from behind the boulder.

FULFILL YOUR SOUL

For the past twenty-five years, I have intentionally chosen to pray with groups of women, or incorporate prayer times into my Bible teaching sessions. I do this because I know that while we sojourn through this life, many boulders will show up in our pathways, and we need help. Prayer is our greatest power. It guides, gives peace, and fulfills beyond anything else this world can provide.

1. Find another person or group of people that will help you find power and fulfillment through prayer. Here is how my friend Sheryl found help:

> *Years ago, I was a young, stressed-out pastor's wife, working a job outside our home while raising a preschooler and kindergartener. Exhausted from the demands of my family and ministry, I was in desperate need of support and friends. God connected me with a Moms In Touch group (now known as Moms in Prayer International). This phenomenal group of women love to pray and taught me how to worship God by praying his names. This practice has deepened my prayer life and increased my faith. I've*

become more acquainted with God's character and thankful to be actively seeking an ever-expanding trust in an almighty God. We can draw close to God by studying his names, but we also draw close to one another through time together in prayer.[75]

2. When an obstacle shows up in your pathway, ask, "God, what are you trying to teach me or show me while I am in the land between?" Then pray faithfully, and wait for God to show you the next steps.

3. One of our biggest struggles is fear. We fear we will never again find happiness, a husband, or a new job; we'll never have a baby, or enough money for retirement. A profound way to find peace and let go of our fear is to follow David's example in Psalms: "In the morning, Lord, you hear my voice; in the morning I lay my requests before you and wait expectantly" (Psalm 5:3 NIV). Waiting expectantly is not wishing something good to happen; it's trusting and believing God will answer your prayer at just the right time.

4. In the same way that I determined to pray for my son for the rest of my life, you must never give up. When you do your part and trust God to do his, your spirit will quiet, your stress will lessen, and you'll be able to move forward with purpose and joy.

5. Give it all to God. Put your hand on your stomach and ask God for healing; ask him to reveal and remove your stress; pray for any forgiveness needed; ask him to eliminate all shame and replace it with the supernatural peace that surpasses all understanding. This type of prayer will set you free.

6. Ask God to reveal any lies Satan has you believing. Pray, asking God to cast out any lies, evil spirits, or assignments of the enemy, and to cover them with the blood of Christ shed on the cross. Ask him to exchange the enemy's work with God's love and peace. Then wait for the sweetness of freedom that fulfills your soul.

S.T.O.P. AND ASK GOD TO HELP YOU
FULFILL YOUR SOUL

BEGIN BY ASKING: *How can I find peace behind my insurmountable obstacle?*

S-Scripture: "Don't worry about anything; instead, pray about everything; tell God your needs and don't forget to thank him for your answers. If you do this you will experience God's peace, which is far more wonderful than the human mind can understand" (Philippians 4:6, 7 TLB).

T-Thanksgiving: "Thank you, God, for caring about all of my needs. Even when I encounter boulders and life seems like a disaster, you are the rock that guides me into peace and a wonderful future."

O-Observation: My life would look a lot different if I was in control. I never imagined that my trouble could be God's mercy in disguise, guiding me into a richer and more fulfilling life and my pathway to peace.

P-Prayer: "God, forgive me for my selfish and negative attitude. Help me to accept my life as it is. Sometimes when I look at the boulders in my pathway, the future seems dark and hopeless. Some days I tremble underneath the weight of stress, disappointment, and hopelessness. So Lord, I give my boulders to you. I yield to your resurrection power in my relationships, my career, my life's purpose, and my hopes and dreams. I will stand fearless and courageous because I choose to put my trust in you. Amen."

CHAPTER 11

FULFILLMENT THROUGH HOSPITALITY

Our Homes, a Haven to Connect Hearts

Love begins at home, and it is not how much we do . . .
but how much love we put in that action.
—MOTHER TERESA

COFFEE SHOPS AND CAFES have a certain allure. The aromatic coffee scent, comfortable ambience, and solace offer people a place to congregate, read, or have a meaningful conversation. These days, coffeehouses serve as a center for something we all crave: social interaction with others. People live busy, hectic lives, and yet make the time to stand in line for their daily fix of caffeine and social connection. But nothing beats having intimate social gatherings with friends right in our homes. Jack and I believe our homes are still the best places to nurture lasting relationships through sharing delicious meals and steaming cups of coffee. Over the years, Jack and I have hosted hundreds of people in our home, so we have endless stories. Here is one of our latest.

The autumn-themed table setting was perfect. Little bundles of Durham wheat, nestled among glass rocks, sparkled in their glass containers. Orange, umber, and brown leaves, and the harvest colors of imitation fruit outlined the table center. Of course, tea lights had to be mixed in with this beautiful décor. Before I stepped onto the deck to mingle with our guests, I took one last look at my delightful table and smiled with satisfaction. I was in deep conversation and enjoying our friends when I heard Jack's panicked voice. "Heidi, quickly come inside; the table is on fire!"

I sprinted into the house to see flames jumping off the napkins, starting on the tablecloth and heading for the wheat. I grabbed the napkins and threw them into the kitchen sink, while Jack used the other napkins to suffocate the flames. None of our guests saw this disaster, so I continued to clean up ashes, replace napkins, and cover the burned holes in the tablecloth. I hoped no one would notice.

But those dark spots couldn't be ignored. As part of the dinner conversation, Jack and I casually replayed the fire disaster. Our guest, Larry, became so curious; he wanted to see if the fire had burned the table. So he lifted the tablecloth. With this seemingly harmless gesture, he tipped over a beautiful, handcrafted water goblet, and shattered glass flew across the table. Shortly afterward, my friend Linda reached for a bun, knocking over her goblet. Her drink spilled over the dazzling white cloth, adding extra red to the Durham wheat. We exploded in laughter. In front of us lay the rubble of burned cloth, ashes, glass, and red spots. Gasping with laughter, we pulled out our phones to capture this disastrous, yet hilarious, moment.

I am convinced that ten years from now, when we get together and relive the evening, no one will remember what we ate. But we will remember the laughter, broken glass, and burned cloth.

WHY HOSPITALITY?

These events in our home are what my husband, Jack, and I call hospitality. This is much different than entertaining. The Greek word for hospitality is *philoxenos*, which comes from *phílos* (love), and *xenos*, (a stranger).[76] This is all about loving those people God places in our lives. When Jack and I married in 1996, we made this declaration:

> *It is our heart's desire to impart the Father's love through word and deed to all those who God places in our lives, knowing that the love which we have received is one of the most precious gifts we can give to others.*

We believe that when we open our homes to others, we offer them a piece of our heart. Our homes are a reflection of our personalities, and when we have Christ's love in us, we display Christ's H-E-A-R-T. Let me break that down.

When we open our homes to others,
we offer them a piece of our heart.

H – Hospitality.

Our homes need to be a haven—a safe harbor, shelter, and sanctuary for family, friends, and guests. The world we live in is confusing, harsh, and demanding. At the end of the day, we all need a welcoming place to set aside our agendas and sink into all that feels safe and comfortable. We need to know it's okay to walk around in bare feet, wash off our make-up, and rummage around the refrigerator for an evening meal.

Most of our hearts also crave beauty, and our homes should reflect the beauty of God's creation. You can fill your homes with fresh flowers or add a plant with twinkling mini-lights. In our home, we have a large, old vase stuffed with mini-lights and topped with seasonal berries. First thing when I walk into our home, I plug in the mini-lights and the ambience in the room lifts my spirit. I become calmer and feel peace. I light some tea candles and put colorful placemats around the table. Those small touches evoke a circle of warmth and family. While the whole outside feels upside down, our homes can still be havens of acceptance, peace, and comfort.

When it is our heart's intention to pour the Heavenly Father's love on guests, they will feel it the minute they walk in the door. It's in the air, in the very spirit that flows out of us. The Bible says, "Most important of all, continue to show deep love for each other, for love makes up for many of our faults. Cheerfully share your home with those who need a meal or a place to stay for the night" (1 Peter 4:8, 9 TLB).

During Jesus' time, there were no fancy Marriott hotels or Trivago to help them find a cheap place to stay. Travelers depended on others to open their homes and offer a hot meal and a warm bed. In our present culture, hospitality is mostly about having people in for meals.

When guests enter our home, what is evident in Jack's and my heart sets the tone. If we are anxious and our intent is to have everything perfect, our guests will pick up our emotions and feel nervous themselves. Conversation will feel forced. Guests need to feel accepted and know:

- It's okay to throw the cushions on the floor and sit by the fireplace.
- In Canada, we often say, "Don't worry about your shoes, leave them on or take them off. Whatever is most comfortable."
- We will pour your first drink, but after that you're on your own.
- Don't worry about the broken glass. We have many more of those tumblers in the cupboard.
- You're welcome to come sit at the kitchen counter while I finish mashing the potatoes.
- You can help me put out the soup bowls.

Mother Teresa lived a great example of what it means to share love in our homes. She once said, "We think sometimes that poverty is only being hungry, naked, and homeless. The poverty of being unwanted, unloved, and uncared for is the greatest poverty. We must start in our own homes to remedy this kind of poverty."[77] By inviting guests to share meals with us, we can feed them and give them acceptance and love. I love the way Nancie Carmichael describes it in her book *Your Life, God's Home.* "I've visited homes where I was made to feel comfortable, welcomed. And there are homes where I've felt that my visit was an intrusion, an inconvenience. What makes a home a shelter rather than a prison? It is an atmosphere of safety, peace, and love. To become a 'house of God'—a place where love dwells—means welcoming people and experiences that God sends my way."[78]

Opening our arms wide and inviting people into our most intimate places, our homes, is the greatest expression of love. Whether you live in a small, humble apartment or a beautifully decorated mansion, if you make it a haven, guests will experience what it means to love one another.

E – Entertaining.

Shiny, slick magazine covers with pictures of exquisite and alluring food creations provide the model for "entertaining." Pinterest and the Master Chef programs on the Food Network set a high bar for preparing meals meant to flaunt and impress. Entertainment looks for payment. It craves words like, "I don't know how you manage to do all this." "You are the most impressive hostess I have ever met." "You have the most beautiful home I have ever seen." Many of today's new homes feature extravagant kitchens, with endless countertops, double ovens, and enormous fridges. Yet many people's lives are too busy to cook or have people over. Meals are often catered, with lavish presentations but little warmth. Our restaurants are full, while our dining rooms and kitchen tables remain empty.

I must confess, we have entertained lavish affairs in our home. During the time my son Donovan was living with us between stints of teaching in Beijing and Singapore, I asked him, "Donovan, if we were to have a party for the release of my book *Sand to Pearls* would you be willing to prepare exotic dishes for about fifty people?" His eyes lit up, and he grabbed paper and started listing creative ideas for fancy appetizers. Donovan is a professor, but his hobby is food. I know how much he loves creating unusual dishes. For the next few weeks, Donovan spent hours planning, preparing shopping lists, and organizing menus and platters. He lovingly prepared exotic dishes of pork belly, seafood, and every manner of appetizer you can imagine. On the evening of the book release, the room overflowed with fresh flowers, candles, and pearls. My daughter Michelle and my granddaughter Mya flew in for the event, and our home was filled with people sipping and sampling the delights. Yes, that was entertaining. For me, the most important aspect was working together with my son—dreaming, preparing, and planning—as our hearts united in love and overflowed with joy.

A – Attitude of Servanthood.

Displaying Christ's heart means being a servant. Jesus spent his years of ministry doing the will of his Father. He modeled what it is to be a servant, to heal people and feed them even when he was tired. In an ultimate example of servanthood, he washed his disciples' feet. In a selfish and inhospitable world, when a person puts someone else's needs before theirs, they provide an oasis of refreshment and encouragement. Serving means offering our homes to people of all races, lifestyles, economic situations, and social barriers. The following story opened my eyes to what it means to have a servant-heart.

> *On June 28, 2005, four Navy SEAL commandos were on a mission in Afghanistan, searching for a notorious al-Qaeda terrorist leader hiding in a Taliban stronghold. As the battle ensued, three of the SEALs were killed, and the fourth, Marcus Luttrell, was blasted unconscious by a rocket grenade and blown over a cliff. Severely injured, he spent the next four days fighting off six al Qaeda assassins who were sent to finish him, and then crawled for seven miles through the mountains before he was taken in by a Pashtun tribe, who risked everything to protect him from the encircling Taliban killers.*
>
> *They took Luttrell back to their village, where the law of hospitality, considered "strictly non-negotiable," took hold. "They were committed to defend me against the Taliban," Luttrell wrote, "until there was no one left alive."[79]*

Wouldn't it be wonderful if we took this Scripture seriously: "Don't forget to be kind to strangers, for some who have done this have entertained angels without realizing it" (Hebrews 13:2 TLB)?

Throughout our married life, Jack and I have tried to model servanthood-hospitality, but it isn't always easy. At times it's been inconvenient, or I've felt tired, wanting to be alone. But each time, we talked about it, and then walked down the hallway to the mission statement that sits in a beautiful frame on a console table. Together we read the last lines of our declaration:

> *Finally, it is our hearts' desire to impart the Father's love through word and deed to all those God places in our lives, knowing that the love which we have received is one of the most precious gifts that we can give to others.*

These words affirm our desire for servanthood, and once again, we'll agree to open our home and embrace whatever God has in store for us. Oftentimes it's a lot of hard work, but it always leaves us fulfilled knowing we invested in the sweetness of richer relationships.

The closer we walk with God, the more he cultivates in us a servant's spirit that is magnetic to others. Servant-hospitality is agreeing to be interrupted and inconvenienced. By following the example of Christ, we silence our own selfish voices and open our hearts to display Christ's love.

Servant hospitality is agreeing to be interrupted and inconvenienced.

R – Rewards.

Hospitality takes pleasure in doing, loving, and serving, with no thought or motive of reward. But rewards do come, when we enter into community with other people. In Jesus' final hours on earth, with the shadow of the cross hanging over him, he spent his last evening sharing dinner with his disciples. Their mouths enjoyed the same food, their bodies reclined around the table, and their eyes met across the plates, creating a place of intimacy.

Then Jesus passed around the bread and wine and told his disciples to eat the bread and drink the wine in remembrance of him

(1 Corinthians 11:24-25, NIV). We now call this service of the Christian discipline "communion." When we partake in it, we are reminded of the reward of receiving all Jesus' blessings here on earth, and the joy and hope of spending eternity with him.

We are rewarded when we "commune" with people by inviting them to live under our roof and share possessions and responsibilities. The apostle Paul wrote, "When God's children are in need, you be the one to help them out. And get into the habit of inviting guests home for dinner, or if they need lodging, for the night" (Romans 12:13 TLB).

Whenever Jack and I are obedient in offering people lodging, we are always amazed and delighted.

- When Scott and Nora Cochrane lived with us for a month, their stimulating conversations refreshed us; they helped take care of our home, and honored our privacy. Nora baked pies for us, a birthday cake, and even cleaned. I know we will have a special connection with them into eternity because of how we communed here on earth.
- Saying yes to a singing group that showed up in ripped jeans, dreadlocks, and sassy t-shirts brought us the love and light of Jesus which outshone their appearance. They brought us music, laughter, and joy that lingered for days.
- While writing this book, a family came for dinner that had previously lived with us for a week when their son Mitchell was eight years old. We laughed and reminisced. *Do you remember the night we were all on our hands and knees cleaning up when Mitchell got so sick?* Going through tough situations with people creates lasting friendships and gives great stories.
- We have shared our guest rooms with people from all over the world, and it has rewarded us with the richness of other cultures, languages, and the knowing that, for some people, we made life a little bit easier and more enjoyable.

Our souls are restless for loving, fun, and intimate human connections. In order to enjoy the fulfillment of these rich experiences, we have to reach deep and open our servant-hearts to make room for people to come and commune with us.

T – Take Time for family meals.

The kitchen is the heart of our home. When my children were little, they sat beside me on the kitchen counter, watching me and stirring the waffle or cake batter. Our kitchen is still a place where we create unusual and delightful dishes. More importantly, it's a place where we chop, laugh, tease, and openly share our love. My children remind me that when they were growing up, they thought it was old-fashioned to have regular family meals, but they have come to realize the powerful benefits. In her book *Surprising Power of Family Meals*, Miriam Weinstein lists some of these benefits.

- Children depend on their parents for the ABCs of good health. Children get 71 percent of their information about how to be healthy from their mothers; 43 percent from their fathers.
- Of teens that have fewer than three family dinners per week, 19 percent report a great deal of tension or stress between family members. This compared to 7 percent of teens who have at least five family dinners per week.
- More mealtime at home was the single strongest factor in better achievement scores and fewer behavioral problems in children of all ages. More meals at home also resulted in less obesity.
- Because feeding is the most basic animal form of caring, sharing meals is one of the most central family bonds.
- Through the mini-lessons of table manners, children learn to share and think of others. By saying "please" and "thank you," we recognize the humanity of our tablemate, acknowledging the fact that we both deserve respect.
- More than a decade of research by The National Center on Addiction and Substance Abuse at Columbia University has found that the more often kids eat dinner with their families, the less likely they are to smoke, drink, or use drugs.[80]

Isn't this information astonishing? Nothing fulfills us like lingering around a dining room table, sharing embellished stories, laughing, or debating relevant topics. Watching the candles burn down while holding a sleeping grandchild on my lap fills me with peace and joy that exceeds any material wealth or success. It illustrates this verse, engraved on the picture on our dining room wall: "They broke bread in their homes and ate together with glad and sincere hearts" (Acts 2:46 NIV).

Eventually, those who did not help with the meal preparation begin the clean up, and the kitchen exudes noise, mess, and chatter. I love what Nancie Carmichael says about the kitchen.

> The kitchen is the heart of the home, the place where we offer food and drink that nourishes us for the journey ahead, restores to us energy we've expended. It's heartwarming to walk into a home filled with the fragrance of a savory stew simmering or bread baking and to see flickering candles. It loudly declares: "This is for you because I care about your most basic needs. I have been planning for you to come because you are loved and wanted here."[81]

When I work in the kitchen, I don't look like June Cleaver in *Leave It To Beaver*,[82] wearing pearls, a starched apron, and hair-sprayed coiffure. But I applaud her effort to create beautiful family mealtimes. My cupboards aren't filled with perfectly lined plates and glasses, and my children tease me about outdated leftovers in the fridge. It's not about perfection, but about the preparation of food, time spent together and love which glues families and friends together.

FULFILL YOUR SOUL

1. I am writing this chapter at the tail end of our Thanksgiving weekend here in Canada. None of our children were able to come home, so we invited friends and others who would otherwise be alone for this family-oriented occasion. Jack and I spent many hours preparing food for fifteen. Keeping with our Thanksgiving tradition, we

told our guests that after dessert, we would ask them to share something they're thankful for. All fifteen guests crowded around the dining room table, and soon the words started to flow. Next came tears, mixed with joyful, intimate, honest expressions of thankfulness. As everyone left, they thanked us for the delicious meal, but mostly for "the most meaningful evening we have enjoyed in a long time." Jack and I went to bed overflowing with joy and fulfillment.

2. You may say, "Maybe that's easy for you, but I don't have the gift of hospitality." May I suggest that each one of us is able to put on the coffee or teapot, sit around a table and engage in heartwarming and honest conversation? When people leave, you will be glad you made the effort.

3. I think some of us feel stress when offering hospitality because of the pressure of trying to measure up to the colorful, exquisite presentations we see on Pinterest, HGTV, and the Food Network. If you love that level of creativity, then enjoy every minute of that process. But, ultimately, what your guests will remember is whether you made them feel accepted and loved.

4. When we treat everyone who comes into our lives as part of the family, we unleash fulfilment. Someday we will all be one large family, sharing intimately in Heaven forever. We can practice that now by inviting people into our havens, sharing our food with them, and making them feel loved. When we offer food and pour love into other's lives, God's reward is mysteriously satisfying.

5. Hospitality creates incredible memories. As we ended our thankful sharing time around the Thanksgiving table, I closed the evening in prayer. I prayed that in the years to come we would remember sitting around this table sharing heartfelt words. Years from now, I know we will remember this defining moment. I know, because I remember when:

- Our barbecuing turkey caught on fire and ended up with a white coating of baking soda and water.
- I fell backward when my chair slipped over a ledge.

- My grandchildren were small, and we collected fruit, grapes, leaves, and dried nuts to decorate our dining room table.
- Someone tipped a candle and it burned up the freeze-dried roses arranged in the middle of the table.

Other people enrich our lives with memories to last a lifetime. We reap what we sow, and if we sow hospitality with love, our blessings and fulfillment become tenfold.

S.T.O.P. AND ASK GOD TO HELP YOU
FULFILL YOUR SOUL

BEGIN BY ASKING: *How can I bring regular mealtime and intimacy back into our home?*

S-Scripture: "They broke bread in their homes and ate together with glad and sincere hearts" (Acts 2:46 NIV).

T-Thanksgiving: "Thank you, God, for a place to lay my head, enjoy a meal, and share my home with those you place in my life. Thank you for this abundant land, where I have enough to share with others."

O-Observation: Our home is not just a home but also a place where people find food, love, acceptance, and even healing. When we eat together with glad and sincere hearts, we may actually be allowing our gift of hospitality to impact and transform someone's life.

P-Prayer: "Thank you, God, that when I share my home, you reward me by fulfilling my soul and enriching my life. Help me to not be afraid to invite people who seem unlovable or different. I ask you to help me carve out deliberate time for family meals so our hearts connect and love and intimacy is restored. Help me be the kind of person who opens her heart and home, welcoming opportunities to share healthy food and the good news of Jesus Christ. Thank you. Amen."

CHAPTER 12

FULFILLMENT THROUGH BEARING WITH ONE ANOTHER

Tow Trucks, Alzheimer's, and Surprising Rewards

The practice of patience toward one another, the overlooking of one another's defects, and bearing of one another is the most elementary condition of all human and social activity in the family, in the professions, and in society.
—LAWRENCE G. LOVASKI

AS SOON AS MY FEET HIT the floor one morning, I started my mental to-do list. I would get through this day as efficiently as possible, so I could blast out of my office and onto the golf course for a 4:57 tee time. Maneuvering my way along the familiar highway, I gasped with joy. The sun was already blazing over the beautiful Okanagan Mountains and vineyards, and the lake shimmered. It was a perfect day for golfing.

As I crested a hill, something startled me and a warning registered in my brain. The black vehicle in front of me was no longer moving. I slammed my foot on the brake, but it was too late. A ghastly crushing noise filled my ears—metal twisting and ripping. The passenger air bag deployed, sending an explosive sound thundering through my little VW Passat. I wondered, *Am I having a heart attack?* My body flew forward, and my chest hurled into the steering wheel. In my confused state, all I could see was smoke and white powder. I knew something terrible had happened.

Miraculously, I managed to dislodge myself from the car. Standing at the side of the road next to the fire truck, ambulance, police cars, and tow trucks, I felt embarrassed and anxious. *My day is ruined. My car is totaled. My joy is gone. I'm going to miss my golf game.* Having caused a traffic jam, I also had to wait there in my linen summer whites, covered in coffee from head to toe, while drivers glared at me. Once I got over my self-absorbed pity party, I became aware of movement around me.

Paramedics checked my eyes, earnestly and kindly asking questions about my well-being. The firemen checked for possible danger of fire, then cleaned up the powder, oil, and mess on the road. While the police checked my registration papers, they asked over and over again, "Madam, are you alright?" The passenger of the vehicle I struck walked over to ask if I was okay. Finally, my wonderful husband showed up and made sure every detail of the accident was attended to and I was looked after. By now my knees were like jelly, I was shaking all over, and I needed every one of these wonderful people to "bear me up" and get me through my ordeal.

We are put on this earth to bear each other's burdens, and I experienced that first-hand. "But Heidi," you might say, "They were just doing their jobs." True, but as followers of Christ we are commanded to do our part to help one another in our troubles.

Share each other's burdens, and in this way obey the law of Christ.
Galatians 6:2 NLT

Bear with each other and forgive one another if any of you has a grievance against someone. Forgive as the Lord forgave you.
Colossians 3:13 NIV

Be completely humble and gentle; be patient,
bearing with one another in love.
Ephesians 4:2 NIV

It is our duty as Christians to help bear each other's burdens. The Greek word for bear in this instance is *bastazo,* which "Signifies to support a burden, to take up, as in picking up anything, stones, to carry something."[83]

*It is our duty as Christians to help bear
each other's burdens.*

We're all just trying to get ahead, restless for peace and joy. We work hard. We worry. We struggle. We have enough troubles of our own and are constantly assaulted with adversities that consume our days. So this concept of carrying someone else's burden runs contrary to our present cultural drift toward more self-absorption in a quest for happiness. We are obsessed with our next entertainment, recreational activity, smart phone upgrade, plus a plethora of tempting diversions. We communicate through Twitter (using 140 characters or less), social-media sound bites, and Instagram, showing the world how successful and busy we are. While pursuing the life we think we deserve, who has time and energy to take on another's problems?

Nevertheless, the apostle Paul said, "For the whole Law can be summed up in this one command: Love others as you love yourself" (Galatians 5:14 TLB). We manifest this command when we bear one another's burdens. The "one another" principles are a practical guide to displaying Christ's love. Jesus bore our burdens at Calvary, and in so doing released you and me from bearing them ourselves. Jesus acted sacrificially, and when we do this for others we become less selfish and more self-sacrificial. This is hardly ever easy, but rewarding and fulfilling in strange and wonderful ways.

BEARING – To Carry Something

Two suitcases accompany me whenever I travel and speak. They always push the fifty-pound limit and they're awkward, heavy, and tiresome. Some of the sweetest and kindest words I hear are, "Can I help you with that?" It lightens my spirit and lessens my physical load—but more importantly, it fills an emotional need. However, when we help someone out of a necessary duty, it can be challenging or hard. Look at the number of people who are caregivers, bearing the burden for an aging population. My sweet friend Kelita is carrying the burden of her mother-in-law's progressive stages of Alzheimer's disease. This is her story:

No one could ever have prepared me for my new role as caregiver to my dear eighty-nine-year-old mother-in-law with Alzheimer's. Sadly, Miss Kitty, as I fondly call her, has become more and more incontinent. A chronic weakness, yes, but sadly another symptom of Alzheimer's. Panty liners, cranberry juice, frequent bathroom visits, lack of water, too much coffee, are much discussed entities and a source of frustration and disdain for my feisty, independent mother-in-law, and me, her controlling, bossy daughter-in-law. She has resisted appropriate assistance for months, and I have been pulling my hair out.

My next job? Sorting through Miss Kitty's pride and joy, her humongous wardrobe. Macular degeneration is taking her eyesight, so spilled soup and gravy stains get missed. Alzheimer's is stealing parts of her brain, so gone are her senses that tell her dirty clothes don't go back into the dresser. So I rush like a mad woman, sorting, folding, and hanging. I act quickly before Miss Kitty makes it back to her room where she finds me invading her closets.

I love my mother-in-law with all my heart, and I have so wanted to do the right thing, but navigating this horrendous disease with her is one of the most difficult and frustrating roles I've ever played. What should be a beautiful act of love, honor, and service, drains out every ounce of patience, good nature, and energy. On days like today, my very worst leaks out, and my heart weeps for what I see in myself.

After a good cry and rant with my husband (after all, it is his mother) and a good night's rest, I awake to face a new day. I promise not to be so hard on myself, to ask for more help when I need it, and to laugh often. Continuing to be humbled, and knowing God has me exactly where he wants me, once again, I surrender.

> *As I hop in my car, and head over to the senior's residence to pick up Miss Kitty for yet another doctor's appointment, I think,* So this is what it's like to serve one another.
>
> *There is nothing easy about carrying other people's messes and hardships. But I know that when I obey the law of Christ to "bear each other's burdens," something happens to me. Knowing I am doing the right thing always empties the selfish and empty parts of my being and satisfies my soul.*[84]

I know many of you are at this stage of life, carrying the burden of your aging parents, neighbors, or children. There is nothing light or easy about the word *burden*. It is defined as a "heavy load, responsibility, difficulty, trouble, strain, duty," and many more hard words. But one day, God will reward you for obeying his command. "He will give each one whatever his deeds deserve" (Romans 2:6 TLB).

BEARING – To support

I must confess that without an end in sight, I am not at my best helping others through their daily drudgery or messes. I'm also not at my best when the person I am trying to help is not making an effort on their part. But I do love to support and mentor women. For over twenty years, I have supported women in their marriages, relationships with their mothers, and even assisted them financially or given them a place to sleep. Janet Thompson, a friend of mine through Advanced Writers and Speakers Association, and founder of Woman to Woman Mentoring, has written several books on mentoring and. here she explains why she does it.

> *Many young women today struggle in their roles in marriage, as mothers, as friends, as employees, as women in the church. Where are the women who will support, selflessly reach out, and "show them the ropes" of living a life in Christ?*
>
> *I've heard the sad testimony of women who walked out of a crusade or revival meeting or the church service where they accepted Christ, and went right back into their old lifestyle. This is tragic*

when there's a wealth of maturity in the women of our churches. There are women who have so much to offer simply because they've grown from walking with Christ and they could help these younger Christian women grow in the Lord too.

Taking the time to reach out to mentor one another is a selfless act of giving and bearing each other's burdens. Not to preach, but teach, love, and support. To let your life—with all the wealth of good and bad experiences—be a role model that Christ was with you through it all. There are women in your church, in your community, in your family . . . who desperately need a woman who will honor the command given to each of us in Titus 2:3–5. Women who will teach how to: study God's Word, be a Christian wife and mother, manage a home and family, deal with temptation or crisis . . . be a 'lady of the Lord.'

Who is assuming responsibility to transmit biblical values to these women? Who is listening to their questions and their concerns and guiding them to the Bible with all the answers and the One who fulfills all our needs?

When we support and make investments in spiritually younger women, it enriches our own lives. The sense of connectedness and shepherding in our church families deepens, society benefits, and we honor God's Word. You can't out-give God. As we share our lives with another sister in Christ, and help to carry their burdens, our own life, and our church will receive immeasurable blessings."[85]

As we share our lives with another sister in Christ, and help to carry their burdens, our own life and our church will receive immeasurable blessings.

Janet goes on to say,

Mentoring is always a two-way, one-another, supporting,

encouraging relationship. If you've experienced the miracles and blessings of being in a Titus 2 mentoring relationship, share your testimony with others who may have questions or be hesitant to mentor. If you've grown spiritually as a mentee, God will put someone in your life who is right where you once were and could use your encouragement and mentoring." [86]

We may live in crowded cities, gated communities, or attend large churches and have people all around us, yet so many individuals are isolated. They have no one to support or share their burdens. We take pride in our independence and love to have control over our own lives. Yet, we are designed to be connected to each other and help each other with our sorrow, anxiety, broken marriages, and other heavy burdens. It's time for all of us, who call ourselves Christians, to lean in, make eye contact, see the sadness and weariness in someone's eyes and ask, "Is there some way I can help you?"

Janet shares my passion for mentoring women because she has experienced the surprising rewards of "miracles and blessings." When we obey God's commands, a supernatural filling takes place in our spirit that cannot be received in any other way.

SURPRISING REWARDS

Miracles and blessings show up in different ways. Through my mentoring relationships I have seen marriages healed, financial burdens lifted, reconciliation between mother and son, healing between mothers and daughters, and women finding more spiritual freedom. I've been blessed and fulfilled beyond my wildest expectations to witness these supernatural miracles. The Bible tells us this is possible.

> "Blessings on you if I return and find you
> faithfully doing your work."
> Matthew 24:46 TLB

"If anyone gives you even a cup of water because you belong to the
Messiah, I tell you the truth, that person will surely be rewarded."
Mark 9:41 NLT

Remember that the Lord will reward each one of us
for the good we do, whether we are slaves or free.
Ephesians 6:8 NLT

It's wonderful when we take the time to help somebody move their
furnishings, give them cash to get through the tough times, or babysit young ones so parents can catch up on their sleep. And one of the
greatest and most practical ways to support someone over an extended
period of time is to be involved in a mentoring relationship. Here are
some of the surprising rewards:

- Our great God is a creator and we are made in his image. When
  we are *creating*, we are doing what we are designed to do and ultimately feel purposeful and fulfilled.
- God planned for a system of order in this world. The Bible says,
  "Older women are to teach the younger women." When we take
  part in God's intentional plan for how things in the world should
  work, our lives are enriched.
- As older women minister to younger women, they pass on the
  wisdom they have learned through their own pain, confusion, and
  failures. When we know our pain it not wasted, but can be used to
  build something beautiful in someone's life, we feel satisfied.
- We "get to" have relationships where we feel accepted, safe, and
  loved. This type of connection fulfills our need for authenticity
  and intimacy.
- We experience joy and awe, watching life transformation before
  our very eyes.
- It causes us to dig into Scripture together, seeking to know God
  more intimately. This way, we both learn.

- It teaches us to pray together and wait for God's answers. Being part of answered prayer is exhilarating and rewarding.
- It teaches us to become vulnerable and honest. Vulnerability opens our hearts to allow another to enter in and explore hidden treasures.
- Mentoring is a mirror for our lives. Modeling Christ to other women causes us to look at ourselves through the eyes of God to see if we are living a godly life.
- Mentoring gives hope, encouragement, love, and wisdom to other women in every stage of their lives. What an awesome opportunity to be used by God to bear someone's burden by being his hands, feet, and voice, and to accomplish his plans and purposes.
- We experience contentment and joy when we know we are obeying the "law of Christ to love one another."

In our restless quest to find fulfillment in this life, most of us struggle with two basic issues: "Who am I?" and "What is my purpose?" In *The Purpose Driven Life*, Rick Warren says, "You were made by God and for God—and until you understand that, life will never make sense . . . You could reach all your personal goals, become a raving success by the world's standards, and still miss the purposes for which God created you."[87]

We discover our roles and purposes in life when we are in relationship with each other, learning to love the way God commanded. Rick goes on to say: "Sometimes it takes years, but eventually you discover that the greatest hindrance to God's blessing in your life is not others, it's yourself—your self-will, stubborn pride, and personal ambition. You cannot fulfill God's purposes for your life while focusing on your own plans."[88]

For the first thirty-two years of my selfish life, my focus was all about my happiness. I didn't understand the contrarian concept that when I make others happy, God ensures that my life is filled with joy. I know God wants to pour good things into our lives, but first we all must learn to allow God's goodness in our lives to flow out to others.

I believe that the small acts of learning to bear one another's burdens lead us away from an unfulfilling, self-absorbed life. The idea is not to think less of us, but to think more of others. God wants to bless us. "For the eyes of the Lord search back and forth across the whole earth, looking for people whose hearts are perfect toward him, so that he can show his great power in helping them" (2 Chronicles 16: 9 TLB).

Will you be a person God can use to bear someone else's burdens? It will rarely be easy. It will take up your time and maybe even your finances. Ultimately, you will be fulfilled and receive delightful, surprising rewards. "Yet this short time of distress will result in God's richest blessing upon us forever and ever!" (2 Corinthians 4:17 TLB).

FULFILL YOUR SOUL

1. When you feel overwhelmed and depleted, it is hard to bear someone else's burdens. In the same way that airline attendants instruct you to put your oxygen mask on before securing it on smaller children, you have to first take care of your heart. Perhaps this chapter will increase your awareness that God created us to help each other and you may be the one that needs to reach out and ask for help. If this is your situation, I ask you to do two things.

   First, the Bible says this about our burdens: "For my yoke is easy to bear, and the burden I give you is light" (Matthew 11:30 NLT). Talk to God, telling him all the burdens you are presently carrying in your own life, and which ones feel wrong or too hard.

   Then, pray and ask God to direct you to someone willing to help you carry some of your load. Sometimes, just telling someone your burdens lightens the load and diffuses anxiety.

2. Determine whether you are "bearing someone's burden" or "enabling."

   Bearing. This is what God commands us to do, to "support a burden." It doesn't mean you are taking over and carrying the whole burden; you are *supporting* it. It means you are there for the person, and you will help them in whatever way you can. You are doing something for them they are not able to do themselves at this time.

Enabling. This means doing things for someone that they can do themselves.

If you have a heart of compassion and mercy, it may be difficult for you to distinguish the difference. But to be kind to yourself and find God's fulfillment while bearing another's burden, you must be able to make the distinction.

3. God will reward your faithfulness when you bear another person's burden. It is a spiritual law that whatever you sow God will reap (Galatians 6:7). If you sow patience and humility and take a step of faith in bearing someone's burden, God will reward you in ways that benefit your life just when you need it.

4. You can bear another's burden in ways that line up with your gifts, abilities, compassion, and schedule. God can take your simple acts and help lift the burden from another's soul:

   • "Weep with those who weep" (Romans 12:15 NLT). So many people are grieving and lonely. Just taking the time to sit or talk with a grieving person helps them to share their burden.
   • Sit with someone who is sick or disabled.
   • Pray. It's a tremendous gift to someone who is hurting.
   • Show up. Offering a cup of coffee, tea, or muffins seems small, but I personally know how significantly this can lighten someone's load.
   • Listen. One of the greatest gifts you can give someone is your ear.

5. Take a bold step and approach a younger woman, asking if you can mentor her. Here are some questions to consider:

   Does she have an authentic desire to be mentored? If the mentee is not serious about learning and growing, both parties eventually become frustrated and realize they are wasting their time.

   Do you really like each other? This may seem like a simple question, but if your personalities are extreme opposites, you'll find it difficult to reach goals and grow together spiritually and intimately.

Do you both have the time and discipline to commit to this?

What is the aim of this relationship? Is it to help someone through a difficult period in her life? Is it to grow spiritually? Is it to learn life skills from another woman?

Do you both know why you are doing this? Talk about all your expectations.

How long is this period of mentoring? Months? One or two years? A season? A lifetime?

Mentoring may just become one of the most fulfilling, enriching tasks you will do as you bear with another person with love.

S.T.O.P. AND ASK GOD TO HELP YOU
FULFILL YOUR SOUL

BEGIN BY ASKING: *Whose burden are you asking me to bear?*

S-Scripture: "Be completely humble and gentle; be patient, bearing with one another in love" (Ephesians 4:2 NIV).

T-Thanksgiving: Thank you, God, that you love me even when I am self-absorbed and oblivious to other people's plights. Thank you for teaching me how to love and live in a way that brings value to this world and enriches my own life.

O-Observation: Some days my own burdens are so heavy, I can't imagine focusing on someone else's. I know that when I seek God's guidance, he is trustworthy to help me find a way to cast my own cares at the cross, so I can be a blessing to someone else.

P-Prayer: "God, first of all, turn the light of truth on my own burdens, so I can hand them over to you. Some days I am not strong enough to carry all that the world demands from me. You tell me in your Word that your "yoke is easy to bear, and the burden I give you is light" (Matthew 11:30 NLT). Help me to remember that your love and purpose for my life is trustworthy, and that you will teach me to yield to the Holy Spirit when life gets tough.

I choose to follow you, even when you take me into uncomfortable and unfamiliar places, for I know that your desire is always to unleash goodness in my life. I ask that you defeat my spirit of selfishness and fear, and help me move forward with determination and courage. Help me fulfill your command to help bear someone else's burden. I thank you in advance for all that you will do through my obedience. Amen."

CHAPTER 13

FULFILLMENT THROUGH LIVING AT PEACE WITH EACH OTHER

The Greatest Gift

*First keep peace with yourself, and then
you can also bring peace to others.*
—THOMAS A. KEMPIS (1380-1471)

WHEN MY GRANDSON ALEX was three years old, all he could talk about was wanting a beautiful swashbuckling sword. I never dreamed that I would help him find this treasure at Old McDonald's Farm while on family vacation in Kelowna, British Columbia. The day of our big adventure arrived, and we were finally buying our admittance tickets. Suddenly, I felt a frantic tugging on my hand. Alex could hardly contain his excitement as he pointed to a box on the floor. "Nana, look at all those swords!" The huge container was full of plastic swords of every color, size, and shape. With his angelic blue eyes and little rosebud mouth, he pleaded, "Nana, if I can have one of these swords, I will be happy for the rest of my life."

My heart melted, and I told him I would buy him whatever sword he desired if he was a good boy for that day. Of course, Alex behaved beautifully, and after three fun-filled hours of petting animals and swimming, we were ready for the box of swords. His eyes darted between his two favorites: the blue sword, and the white one. Finally he decided, and said, "Okay, Nana, I'll take the blue one." We made the purchase and he happily skipped out to the parking lot.

Before we had even arrived at my car, he looked at me with pleading eyes and said, "Nana, I really want the *white* one." Too late. The blue one had been purchased. He cried all the way home. Even though it broke my heart, I felt he needed to learn early in life the consequences of making choices.

A year later, we were visiting Alex's family on Vancouver Island, and I asked him if he would like to come along on an errand. I strapped him into his car seat, and as we were driving down the highway, I heard his timid little voice, "Nana, I really wanted the *white* one!" Our eyes met in the rearview mirror, and I had to look away because tears welled up in my eyes. If he would have whined and demanded the white sword, it would have been a different story. But what I really heard him say was, "Nana, you did not hear the deep longing in my heart."

Months passed, and I was in the middle of my Christmas shopping when I spotted it. A perfect *white* sword. I bought it, took it home, and wrapped it up tenderly so that my little Alex would find this precious gift under the Christmas tree. I wanted him to have his magical white sword. He never demanded it, but in his quiet way he told me the desires of his heart. I wanted him to know his request was significant enough for me to hear.

Fast forward nine years. Alex flew out to Kelowna to spend a week with us and participate in a summer soccer program. During one supper hour, while Alex was devouring his favorite meal of shrimp and pasta, I asked him, "So Alex, are you still the happiest boy on Earth because I bought you the white sword?" With a puzzled look on his face, he replied, "Nana, what in the world are you talking about?" I smiled, knowing that since then, there had been many other things that he thought would make him happy for the rest of his life. Our restless natures often want something so badly that we are convinced it will make us happy forever. But happiness is fickle. Very quickly we want more, bigger, and better.

My love for my grandson Alex is like God's love for me. God knows the deepest longings of my heart, and he wants to give me the kind of gifts that will bring me the most joy. He also knows that what the world has to offer will only give me fleeting pleasure, so he offers me the greater gifts—those that will satisfy every fiber of my being and every corner of my soul. Before Jesus went to the cross, he said he would leave us the greatest gift. "I am leaving you with a gift—peace of mind and heart! And the peace I give isn't fragile like the peace the world gives. So don't be troubled or afraid" (John 14:27 TLB).

Where does a person find that kind of peace in the midst of sorrow and challenges, in our fast-paced and confusing world?

The Bible says that we can have "peace in our minds." Can we actually have peace as we think about our daily tasks, school meetings, grocery lists, bills to be paid, cars to be filled with gasoline, and myriad other distractions that come at us like scud missiles? It also says we can have "peace of heart," which includes harmony and absence of hostility in our relationships, when we release all unforgiveness, resentment, jealousy, and anger. That seems too good to be true. But that is the kind of peace God is ready to give us when we ask him to come and rule in our lives. The Greek word for peace is *eirḗnē* (from, *eirō*, "to join, tie together into a whole")—properly, *wholeness*, i.e., when all essential parts are joined together; *peace* (God's gift of *wholeness*).[89] Wholeness in every area.

While I am writing this chapter, it's a gorgeous autumn day in Kelowna, British Columbia. I'm surrounded by flowers on my deck in brilliant shades: tangerine geraniums, white bacopa, pink oleander, vines cascading beyond their pots. Through my office window, I view the Okanagan Lake in its entire splendor, and today the water is smooth as glass and sparkling like diamonds. Even though my office is full of books, files, and stacks of papers, all my deadlines have been met. My relationships are all in order. I had a good sleep last night. I even went for a five-kilometer walk this morning, and my new activity tracker, the FitBit on my arm, tells me I had an exceptional day. When I have one of these "wholeness" paradise days, I am content, and it's easy to spread peace wherever I go. I long to capture this moment and revel in this contentment—because it isn't always like this.

Peace is an exquisite sensation. But we can't depend on our outer circumstances to give us this feeling. We live in the tension of meeting our daily challenges: dropping children off at school, taking the dog to the vet, sitting at traffic lights, being stuck on the phone for hours solving technical problems, hockey practices, and on and on. By the time it's dark outside, we've had enough of everything and everyone, and we just want to curl up and be left alone.

We'll never find peace if we wait for the world to hand it to us. Even if we plan our lives very carefully, the distractions will never disappear, the lists will never end, and the tension will always be there. We crave peace, an earthly reflection of paradise. So what happened?

---

*We'll never find peace if we wait
for the world to hand it to us.*

PARADISE LOST

Adam and Eve had life at their fingertips. They never knew fear, worry, or stress. They experienced paradise in exquisite ways we will never understand. What would make them sabotage that? They were tempted and taunted into believing that God was holding something back that would make life even better (Genesis 3:1–6). The lust of the eyes and the restless craving for something *more* eventually brought disappointment and pain. Sure enough, immediately after they disobeyed God's command, Adam and Eve felt shame about being naked. Their beautiful innocence and the wholehearted peace they had enjoyed with God and each other was gone.

Adam and Eve are our spiritual ancestors. We share their story and mirror their lives. We are selfish, disobedient, and never satisfied. Instead of allowing God to rule our lives, we spend too much time trying to be right and attempting to control our circumstances so we can have what we want. We were meant to live in peace with God, with our neighbors, and with ourselves. Instead we live inside a broken paradise.

GIVE ME BACK MY PEACE

God never gives up on us, and he wants to restore our earthly paradise. Thousands of years ago, while the shepherds were taking care of their sheep, there was glorious jubilation when they heard heavenly hosts declare: "'Glory to God in the highest heaven,' they sang, 'and peace on earth for all those pleasing him'" (Luke 2:1 TLB). Christ came into the world to restore our peace so that our story can become his story. The apostle Paul sacrificed his life to declare, "For Christ himself is our way of peace" (Ephesians 2:14 TLB),

The older I get, the more I realize that peace truly is God's greatest gift to me. But our enemy, Satan, slyly and relentlessly attempts to steal everything good God provides for his children. Peace is our richest gift, so obviously Satan will do everything he can to prevent us from enjoying it.

To enjoy a life of peace, I have to constantly examine my life to see what is robbing me of it. I am stronger, more alert, and better able to make good choices when I've had good night's sleep. Satan knows I'm vulnerable when I am tired, and over the years he has especially tried to sabotage my sleep and my joy before I fly out to speak at a conference. My sleep will always be interrupted by some mishap, a sore throat, or a last-minute crisis. I have to remain aware of my vulnerabilities and observe what robs my peace in every area of my life.

- When, in the middle of a stressful day, I have another unwelcome interruption.
- When I have to spend time on the phone to resolve a technical problem.
- When I must wait endlessly in a long line-up because of a chatty clerk.
- When I'm tired and someone asks me another question.
- When someone embarrasses me and makes me feel stupid.

It helps to know what bothers us. Becoming familiar with our annoyances and how they frustrate us helps us decide how we will deal with them. We can't maintain peace simply by human, fleshly efforts. We try and fail, get angry or frustrated, and fail and try again. We need the strength, wisdom, and power of the Holy Spirit to reveal the things we simply need to endure and to be empowered to tackle the things we need to change.

This topic of peace is very tender, because for a period of five years, my life was especially difficult. For many years, my sister Brigitte and

I attended to my ailing mother's needs, but over time it became increasingly challenging. Her blood condition required frequent time-consuming, laborious visits to the doctor's office and blood clinics. For the four years leading up to her death, my mother loved it when Brigitte and I helped her with grocery shopping, attended to her personal needs, or just sat and talked with her. During the last year of her life, I was also in crisis mode. In my job as controller for two car dealership franchises, I had to figure out a new dealership management computer program. Despite training people, running my ministry, serving as a pastor's wife, mother, stepmother, and nana, I still strove to be the dutiful daughter. Most mornings, before my feet hit the floor, my mind rifled through the day's obligations and my peace vanished instantly. I stayed awake many nights, praying, seeking wisdom, asking God for help, and trying to figure out how I was going to handle the coming day's activities. Most of the time, peace eluded me.

There comes a time when we have to make drastic changes in order to reclaim the gift of peace. On January 2, 2014, I woke up and listened to the Holy Spirit nudging me to quit my job. I could hardly wait to get to the office and deliver the news. For the first time in four years, I felt peace flood through my soul, heart, and mind. The gift of peace was back, and I embraced it with amazement and delight. I stayed on at the dealership for another year, but throughout that time I still felt at peace because an end was in sight. My retirement date of March 5, 2015, finally arrived, and my heart continues to overflow with joy. It's clear that we need to listen to the nudging of the Holy Spirit and do our part in pursuing *eirō* (wholeness), to enjoy a peaceful life.

There comes a time when we have to make drastic changes in order to reclaim the gift of peace.

When I allow the Prince of Peace (Isaiah 9:6) to have dominion over my soul, and lean in to listen and obey, Jesus guides me into reclaiming his greatest gift. If I don't have peace in my heart, I don't have any to pass on to others.

GET JESUS INTO THE BOAT

Often we are unhappy and we lose our peace because of our poor choices or tough circumstances. We feel stuck. But sometimes life just happens. We are in the middle of a storm, and we need Jesus to get into the boat with us. That is what happened when my first husband, Dick, died. My grief was painful and deep, and my pounding heart sabotaged my appetite and sleep. I only wanted one thing—peace. For weeks, I walked around the house repeating one simple prayer, "Jesus please give me peace. I need peace. I just want peace."

Initially, peace came in snippets. But I needed more. Whenever anyone asked if they could help me, I always responded: "Please pray that I will have peace." Soon, peace stayed a little longer. Eventually, I was able to sleep, eat regular meals, and regain my strength. Going through that horrific season made me acutely aware that in the middle of my storms, I can't help myself. I need the Prince of Peace to come and rule in every fiber of my being. In his book *The Me I Want to Be,* John Ortberg describes it this way: "The peace of Jesus is something much deeper than self-help techniques to manage stress. It is deeper than anxiety reduction to make life more pleasant. It is the settled conviction that goes down to the core of your being—to your belly where rivers of living water can flow—that all things are in God's hands. Therefore all things will be well, and you can live free of worry, burden, and fear."[90]

We can't have peace without knowing that Jesus is the lover of our soul, that we can trust him with our lives, and that he is always there to climb into our boats and help us navigate treacherous storms.

PEACE WITH EACH OTHER

Back in the sixties and seventies, an upside-down Y in a circle was the peace symbol prominently displayed on jewelry, concrete walls, and telephone poles. This well-known image shouted to the world to stop our wars and fighting, and start getting along with each other.

Believers look at the cross as a symbol of sacrificial blood, shed so we can live without condemnation for our sin. So we *can* have peace.

Imagine what this world would look like if we all made room for the peace of Christ to rule our hearts and minds. Marriages would heal; wars and political mudslinging would end. Our lives would be satisfying and we would feel happy. Scripture tells us, "Be happy. Grow in Christ. Pay attention to what I have said. Live in harmony and peace. And may the God of love and peace be with you" (2 Corinthians 13:11 TLB). Here are some ways to live with others, enjoying fulfillment through harmony and peace. "Be humble and gentle. Be patient with each other, making allowance for each other's faults because of your love. Try always to be led along together by the Holy Spirit, and so be at peace with one another" (Ephesians 4:2 TLB).

Be humble and gentle. These words sound weak, but in fact they are strong because they refer to deliberate choices. We are to consider others better than ourselves. We can only do this when we know Christ is at the center of our lives, and he will give us strength and courage when we need it. Gentleness diffuses wrath and harsh words, restoring peace and harmony.

Be patient with each other. None of us is without defects. We need to be tolerant of each other's shortcomings and foibles. When our schedules are stretched tight, it's hard to be patient and express tolerance with people who are contrary to our nature. We need to make room to listen to each other, and see life from the others person's perspective. Patience means having mercy with others in the same way that Christ has mercy with us.

Be gracious. When Jack and I play golf, we occasionally give each other *mulligans.* I love it when someone overlooks my mistake, pats me on the back and says, "No worries, Sister. Don't give it a second thought." It's money in the bank for the next time they mess up.

Be led by the Holy Spirit. None of the above ideas will work if we don't allow the power and wisdom of the Holy Spirit to quicken our hearts when we have spoken hurtful, judgmental words. We need the

Holy Spirit to reveal the log in our own eyes, so we can be quick to forgive, put an end to criticizing, and express love—so peace is restored.

Be at peace with one another. Dietrich Bonhoeffer must have exuded many of these qualities while he was in prison for his staunch resistance to the Nazi dictatorship and genocidal persecution of the Jews. A German Lutheran pastor, theologian, and key founding member of the Confessing Church, Bonhoeffer became imprisoned in 1943. Later transferred to a Nazi concentration camp, he was executed by hanging just two weeks before Allied forces liberated the camp and three weeks before Hitler's suicide. After his execution, his fellow prisoners described him: "Many of his fellow prisoners who survived the war would later recall Dietrich's peaceful demeanor during this time and remark on how calm he was. They would remember how encouraging he was to those who were better off than he, and how resolute he was in his simple faith toward God. In the worst of all circumstances, he had resigned himself to God's will and had found an inward contentment."[91]

Bonhoeffer was able to live in peace because he had something we all need. We must first have peace *with* God before we can experience the peace *of* God. We receive peace from God by accepting his gift—the blood that Jesus shed at Calvary for the forgiveness of our sins, and the glorious hope of eternal life. Then that peace is appropriated through the indwelling and release of the Holy Spirit. What a great gift!

SHOES OF PEACE

Many people don't realize they're experiencing dissatisfaction and restlessness because they lack this peace. We need to help one another walk in the shoes of Christ and find this great gift. "For shoes, put on the peace that comes from the Good News so that you will be fully prepared" (Ephesians 6:15 NLT).

But we live in a distorted world, so we must be careful not to confuse peace*making* with peace*keeping*.

1. Peacemaker. Jesus said, "Blessed are the peacemakers, for they will be called children of God" (Matthew 5:9 NIV). Peacemakers create peace and harmony through honesty and speaking the truth in love. Instead of hostility, resentment, and anger, they own their mistakes and choose to pray for forgiveness and ultimate reconciliation. We must do whatever we can to bring peace into our areas of influence. Mother Teresa said, "If we have no peace, it is because we have forgotten that we belong to each other."[92]

2. Peacekeeper. This is when people walk on eggshells trying not to offend anyone. They whitewash tension, are dishonest about their feelings, and avoid conflict at any cost. They equate being passive with keeping peace. But they can't *keep* peace that doesn't exist.

Yes, you and I need to do our part in organizing our circumstances and making the good decisions that will enhance our life and bring us joy. But God's peace is an inside job that only Christ can give. "And the peace of God, which transcends all understanding, will guard your hearts and your minds in Christ Jesus" (Philippians 4:7 NIV). After the death of my husband, I could not orchestrate my life to bring me peace except through Christ, flowing through the Holy Spirit. It's real, and it's available to anyone who believes in the power of Christ.

FULFILL YOUR SOUL

God may not want us to have every "magical" white sword we desire, because he knows that's not where lasting joy comes from. But he does want us to have the lasting and fulfilling gift of peace. We need to diligently protect our peace, because Satan never stops trying to deceive and steal anything good God provides for His children.

As situations arise that threaten to rob us, it is important we appropriate Christ's peace. Here are several ways:

1. We lose our peace when we are in a crisis situation or if there is tension in a relationship. We can hear Satan taunting us: "Well, what are you going to do about this?" "Can you handle this?" "This

is going to ruin you." "She never liked you in the first place." It is true, frequently we don't know what to do and Satan likes to make us think we will fail. But we are not meant to handle all of life's problems. We are to look to the Holy Spirit for wisdom, to know and believe that God will see us through any difficult situation. Jesus said that in this world we will find trouble (John 16:33), but when we fix our eyes on him, he will help us to walk on the water and not drown.

2. Learn to "shake off" rejection. When the apostle Paul was on the island of Malta, helping people build a fire, a poisonous viper crawled out from under a pile of brushwood and fastened itself on his hand (Acts 28:2–5). Paul shook the snake, and it fell into the fire, causing him no harm. This is how we must deal with the searing pain of rejection. We must allow the Holy Spirit to help us shake off offenses and words that hurt us so we don't lose our peace. When others see that we are able to have peace and remain calm during "viper bites," they will want to know where our peace comes from.

3. We must learn to trust God in every circumstance. We may think that alcohol, food, a new relationship, or drugs will help us solve the problem. But it won't. When we wake up, the problem will still be there, and no one can help us but God. "The good man does not escape all troubles—he has them too. But the Lord helps him in each and every one" (Psalm 34:19 TLB).

4. Recognize the traps. Satan sets people up to misunderstand each other so he can separate and divide marriages, friendships, churches, and governments. We need to be careful not to misinterpret conversations or assume unrealistic expectations. Don't be too shy to ask, "Is this what I heard you saying?" We don't want to lose our harmony, for then we lose our peace. "Let the peace of Christ keep you in tune with each other, in step with each other" (Colossians 3:15 MSG).

5. Peace is a fruit of the Holy Spirit. When we receive Jesus Christ as our personal Savior, we receive the gift of peace. Peace doesn't mean the absence of fear, turmoil, pain, and grief. Peace is promised in the middle of our storms.

S.T.O.P. AND ASK GOD TO HELP YOU
FULFILL YOUR SOUL

BEGIN BY ASKING: *How can I have peace in the middle of the night, when I feel alone and anxious?*

S-Scripture: "Do not be anxious about anything, but in everything, by prayer and petition, with thanksgiving, present your requests to God. And the peace of God, which transcends all understanding, will guard your hearts and your minds in Christ Jesus" (Philippians 4:6, 7 NIV).

T-Thanksgiving: "Thank you, God, for peace. I know that in the middle of my troubles and hardship the greatest gift you give me is peace."

 O-Observation: It's horrible when I wake up in the middle of the night to the pounding of my heart and thoughts in my head that keep repeating, "So now what are you going to do?" In my human, fragile state, I don't always know how to resolve complicated problems, and I often find I have only questions and no answers. When it is dark and lonely, I know God is the only one who can help me. He is the Prince of Peace and he wants rule over my heart.

P-Prayer: "God, the burdens in my heart are lifted and my hands are raised in praise. I surrender all my worries, anxieties, and fear. Teach me how to rest in your presence and trust you for my future, so I can enjoy the greatest gift—peace. Rule in my heart during my greatest trials, and turn on the light of truth so I can learn to trust you in every circumstance. I am not strong or wise enough to run my own life; I need your Holy Spirit to give me assurance and wisdom and fill me with the sweetness and contentment of peace. Thank you that you will. Amen."

EPILOGUE

IN OUR QUEST for find fulfillment and joy, our biggest obstacles are our daily distractions. It is my greatest desire that you find the sweet fulfillment God designed all of us to enjoy. But we must remember to S.T.O.P. and do two crucial things.

Most importantly, pray and ask Jesus, the Son of God, to forgive you from all of your past sins. All the bad things you have done in your life carry a lot of negative power over you, and they'll keep you on a treadmill seeking fleeting happiness. But when you confess your sins to God, he forgives every one of them. Here's a promise: "But if we confess our sins to him, he can be depended on to forgive us and to cleanse us from every wrong" (1 John 1:9 TLB). What would that prayer do? It reconnects you with your creator, God. Please pray this simple prayer with me.

> *Father,*
>
> *You loved the world so much that you gave your only begotten Son to die for my sins, that I would not perish but have everlasting life. I believe and confess with my mouth that Jesus Christ is your Son, the Savior of the world. I believe he died on the cross for me and bore all my sins, paying the price for them. I acknowledge that I have sinned, and ask you to please forgive me. Fill me with the Holy Spirit and give me the gift of eternal life. Be my power, by giving me the mind of Christ to help me on the pathway to embracing the glorious and fulfilling life you created for me.*
>
> *Thank you that you will. Amen.*

You can try harder, act differently, be nicer, be less busy, focus on relationships, and criticize less, but eventually you will find that without God's forgiveness and power in your life, you're still restless.

Second, now that God has forgiven all your sins, you must turn around and forgive everyone who has hurt you. This is not a nice, easy option, but the Bible commands us to forgive. "Be gentle and ready to forgive; never hold grudges. Remember the Lord forgave you, so you must forgive others" (Colossians 3:13 TLB).

In all sincerity, I tell you that forgiving everyone in my life has set me free from the hooks of shame, guilt, anger, and resentment. I will be in this transformation process for the rest of my life, but everyday God refills me with the beautiful fruit of the Spirit: love, joy, peace, patience, and all the other qualities that saturate my soul with fulfillment. I want you to know this fulfillment as well.

When I walk people through process of forgiveness, I use the following steps. In order to do a complete, supernatural heart work, I suggest you go through all of them with each person you need to forgive.

1. On a sheet of paper, write down the names of the people who have hurt or offended you.
2. Face the hurt and the hate. Write down how you feel about these people and their offenses.
3. Acknowledge that Jesus died for your sins.
4. Decide you will bear the burden of each person's sin. All true forgiveness is substitutionary, as was Christ's forgiveness of us.
5. Decide to forgive. Forgiveness is a conscious choice to let the other person off the hook, which frees you from the past. The feelings of freedom will eventually follow.
6. Take your list to God: "God, I choose to forgive (name) for (list of offenses: what they did and how it made you feel)."
7. Destroy the list. You are now free.
8. Let go of expectations that your forgiveness will result in major changes in the other person.
9. Try to understand the people you have forgiven. They are also victims.

10. Expect positive results of forgiveness in yourself. In time, you will be able to think about the people who have offended you without hurt, anger, or resentment.
11. Thank God for the lessons you have learned and for setting you free.
12. Be sure to accept your part of the blame for the offenses you suffered.
13. Do something to bless the person who hurt you.

Forgiveness is difficult, and feelings of joy and freedom may take longer than you think. Please persevere. If someone hurt you deeply, you may have to pray many times until the ugly hook is completely released from your heart. One day, you will be able to look that person in the eye and bless them. Then you'll know you've experienced the powerful transformation from illusions of struggling to create your ideal life, to living with true joy and fulfillment.[93]

Connect with
Heidi McLaughlin

*Heidi uses her passion and gifts of speaking and writing
in her ministry called Heart Connections.
To download your free* Restless for More *group study guide,
or to book Heidi to speak at your next event, please visit:*

www.heartconnection.ca

Or write to her at:
Heidi McLaughlin
1529 Chardonnay Place
West Kelowna, British Columbia
V4T 2P9 Canada
Phone: 1-250-470-9299

Blog: www.heartconnection.ca
Facebook: heidi.mclaughlin.7
Twitter: heidiheart

Notes

Chapter 1

1 Bill Hybels, *Simplify: Ten Practices to Unclutter Your Soul,* (Tyndale Momentum, An Imprint of Tyndale House Publishers, Inc., 2014), 12.

2 http://www.cdc.gov/features/dssleep, June 15, 2015.

3 http://www.cdc.gov/features/dssleep, June 15, 2015.

4 http://www.blueletterbible.org/lang/Lexicon/Lexicon.cfm?strongs=H7665&t=KJV.

5 http://www.blueletterbible.org/lang/Lexicon/Lexicon.cfm?strongs=G2168&t=KJV.

6 http://www.blueletterbible.org/lang/Lexicon/Lexicon.cfm?strongs=G5485&t=KJV.

7 http://www.blueletterbible.org/lang/Lexicon/Lexicon.cfm?strongs=G5479&t= KJV.

8 http://www.biblegateway.com/passage/?search=Romans+16%3A25%2CEphesians+3%3A20&version=ESV.

9 Jeff Manion, *Satisfied, Discovering Contentment in a World of Consumption* (Grand Rapids, Michigan: Zondervan, 2013), 47, 48.

Chapter 2

10 John Ortberg, *The Me I Want to Be: Becoming God's Best Version of You* (Grand Rapids, Michigan: Zondervan, 2010), 13.

11 Mark Buchanan, *Hidden In Plain Sight, The Secret of More* (Nashville, Tennessee: Thomas Nelson, 2007), 14.

12 Katie Brazelton, *Pathway to Purpose for Women* (Grand Rapids, Michigan: Zondervan, 2005), 153.

13 Rick Warren, *The Purpose Driven Life, What On Earth Am I Here For?* (Grand Rapids, Michigan: Zondervan, 2002), 242.

14 Used with permission from Joanne Bonk.

15 Geri Scazzero, *The Emotionally Healthy Woman, Eight Things you Have to Quit to Change Your Life* (Grand Rapids, Michigan: Zondervan, 2010), 153.

16 Joel Osteen, *Your Best Life Now, 7 Steps To Living At Your Full Potential* (New York, New York: Time Warner Book Group, 2004), 76.

Chapter 3
17 Rick Warren, *The Purpose Driven Life* (Grand Rapids, Michigan: Zondervan, 2002), 64.

18 Skye Jethani, *WITH, Reimagining The Way You Relate to God* (Nashville: Tennessee: Thomas Nelson, 2011), 39.

19 http://en.wikipedia.org/wiki/Bienenstich. Bienenstich or Bee sting cake is a German dessert made of a sweet yeast dough with a baked-on topping of caramelized almonds and filled with a vanilla custard, Buttercream or cream.

Chapter 4
20 http://www.blueletterbible.org/lang/Lexicon/Lexicon.cfm?strongs=H3045&t= KJV.

21 Ruth Haley Barton, *Sacred Rhythms, Arranging our Lives for Spiritual Transformation* (Downers Grove, Illinois: InterVarsity Press, 2006), 36.

22 Dallas Willard, *The Great Omission, Reclaiming Jesus's Essential Teachings on Discipleship* (New York, New York: HarperCollins, 2006), 69.

23 Dallas Willard, *The Great Omission, Reclaiming Jesus's Essential Teachings on Discipleship* (New York, New York: HarperCollins, 2006), 131.

24 Linda Evans Shepherd, *Experiencing God's Presence, Learning to Listen While You Pray* (Grand Rapids, Michigan: Revell, a division of Baker Publishing Group, 2013), 111.

25 David G. Benner, *Surrender To Love, Discovering the Heart of Christian Spirituality* (Downers Grove, Ilinois: InterVarsity Press, 2003), 22.

26 http://www.todayschristianwoman.com/articles/2010/september/needsilence-solitude.html, July 28, 2015.

27 Rick Warren, *The Purpose Drive Life, What on Earth Am I Here For?* (Grand Rapids, Michigan: Zondervan, 2002), 24.

Chapter 5

28 http://www.blueletterbible.org/lang/Lexicon/Lexicon.cfm?strongs=G3875&t= KJV, July 21, 2015.

29 Larry Crabb, *Connecting, Healing for Ourselves and our Relationships* (Nashville, Tennessee: Word Publishing, 1997), 31.

30 Jeff Manion, *Satisfied, Discovering Contentment in a World of Consumption* (Grand Rapids, Michigan: Zondervan, 2013), 74.

31 http://www.eoht.info/page/Nature+abhors+a+vacuum, August 11, 2015.

32 Brene' Brown, *Daring Greatly* (New York, New York: Penguin Group (USA) Inc., 2012), 23.

33 Dr. Archibald D. Hart & Dr. Sylvia Hart Frejd, *The Digital Invasion, How Technology is Shaping You and Your Relationships* (Grand Rapids, Michigan: Baker Books, 2013), 99.

34 Ibid., 101.

35 Ibid., 124.

36 Ibid., 111.

37 Ibid., 112.

38 Bill Hybels, *Simplify,:Ten Practices to Unclutter Your Soul* (Carol Stream, Illinois: Tyndale House Publishers, 2014), 59.

39 Brene Brown, *Daring Greatly* (New York, New York: Penguin Group (USA) Inc., 2012), 80.

40 http://www.goodreads.com/quotes/139677-the-greatest-disease-in-the-west-today-is-not-tb, August 11, 2015.

41 http://www.amazon.com/Love-Beyond-Reason-John-Ortberg-ebook/ dp/B003JH82SS/ref=sr_1_2?s=books&ie=UTF8&qid=1439594619&sr=1-2&keywords=LOVE+BEYOND+REASON, August 14, 2015.

Chapter 6

42 Joel Osteen, *Your Best Life Now, 7 Steps To Living At Your Full Potential* (New York, New York: Warner Faith Time Warner Book Group, 2004), 139.

43 Larry Crabb, *Connecting, Healing from Ourselves and Our Relationships* (Nashville, Tennessee: Word Publishing, 1997), 131.

44 http://www.blueletterbible.org/lang/Lexicon/Lexicon.cfm?strongs=G3870&t= KJV, August 30, 2015.

45 The name Linda has been changed for anonymity.

46 http://www.blueletterbible.org/lang/Lexicon/Lexicon.cfm?strongs=G3618&t= KJV, September 2, 2015.

47 Rick Warren, *The Purpose Driven Life, What on Earth Am I Here for* (Grand Rapids, Michigan: Zondervan, 2002), 242.

48 Priscilla Shirer, *The Resolution for Women* (Nashville, Tennessee: B&H Publishing Group, 2011), 125.

49 http://www.newyorker.com/science/maria-konnikova/power-touch, September 3, 2015.

Chapter 7

50 http://www.oneplace.com/ministries/love-worth-finding, September 12, 2015.

51 http://experiencelife.com/article/the-power-of-kindness, September 12, 2015.

52 http://ns.umich.edu/new/releases, 7724, September 12, 2015.

53 http://ns.umich.edu/new/releases, 7724, September 12, 2015.

54 http://biblehub.com/greek/5544.htm, September 12, 2015.

55 Used with permission from Captain Rachele Lamont – The Salvation Army, *Heather is not her real name.

56 http://www.huffingtonpost.com/project-compassion-stanford/the-healing-power-of-kindness_b_6136272.html, September 12, 2015.

57 http://www.vatican.va/news_services/liturgy/saints/ns_lit_doc_20031019_madre-teresa_en.html, September 14, 2015.

58 Mother Teresa - https://en.wikipedia.org/wiki/File:President_Reagan_presents_ Mother_Teresa_with_the_Medal_of_Freedom_1985.jp, September 14, 2015.

59 Used with permission from Jack McLaughlin.

60 Joel Osteen, *Your Best Life Now, 7 Steps To Living At Your Full Potential* (New York, New York: Warner Faith Time Warner Book Group, 2004), 242.

Chapter 8

61 Joel Osteen, *Your Best Life Now, 7 Steps To Living At Your Full Potential* (New York, New York: Warner Faith, Time Warner Book Group, 2004), 40.

62 http://alikennedylive.com/2011/05/03/honoring-our-parents-three-reasons-why-this-command-shouldnt-be-ignored, October 19, 2015.

63 John Bevere, *Honor's Reward, How To Attract God's Favor And Blessing* (New York, New York: FaithWords Hachette Book Group, 2007), 209.

64 Used with permission from Larry Dieno, August 25, 2015.

Chapter 9

65 http://www.sabbathchurch.org/bara-creation.html, June 22, 2015.

66 Joseph Cavanaugh III, *The Language of Blessing* (Tyndale Momentum, An Imprint of Tyndale House Publishers, Inc., 2013), 11, 15.

67 http://www.charismamag.com/life/family-parenting/15245-speaking-blessings-upon-your-children, June 22, 2015.

68 http://sljinstitute.net/pentateuch/genesis/jacob-blessing-josephs-sons, June 15, 2015

69 http://sljinstitute.net/pentateuch/genesis/jacob-blessing-josephs-sons, June 15, 2015.

Chapter 10

70 Bill Hybels, *Too Busy Not To Pray, Slowing Down to Be with God* (Downers Grove, Illinois: InterVaristy Press, 2008), 158.

71 Bill Hybels, *Too Busy Not To Pray, Slowing Down to Be with God* (Downers Grove, Illinois: InterVaristy Press, 2008), 158.

72 Mark Batterson, *The Circle Maker, Praying Circles Around Your Biggest Dreams and Greatest Fears* (Gale, Cengage Learning, 2011), 157.

73 Used with permission from Dr. Saundra Dalton-Smith. http://ichoosemybestlife.com, October 30, 2015.

74 http://en.wikipedia.org/wiki/War_Room_(film), October 30, 2015.

75 Used with permission from Sheryl Giesbrecht. http://fromashestobeauty.com, October 30, 2015.

Chapter 11

76 http://remnantreport.com/cgi-bin/imcart/read.cgi?article_id=297&sub=10, October 6, 2015.

77 http://www.brainyquote.com/quotes/quotes/m/mothertere130839.html, October 6, 2015.

78 Nancie Carmichael, *Your Life, God's Home, Knowing the Joy of His Presence* (Wheaton, Illinois: Crossway Books, 1998), 148.

79 http://www.sermoncentral.com/illustrations/sermon-illustration-austin-mansfield-stories-hospitality-doinggodswill-62630.asp, October 6, 2015.

80 http://poweroffamilymeals.com/resources/about, October 13, 2015.

81 Nancie Carmichael, *Your Life, God's Home, Knowing the Joy of His Presence* (Wheaton, Illinois: Crossway Books, 1998), 146.

82 http://www.imdb.com/title/tt0050032, October 13, 2015.

Chapter 12

83 *Vines Expository Dictionary of New Testament Words* (Iowa Falls, Iowa: Riverside Book and Bible House), 92.

84 With permission from Kelita Haverland, http://www.kelita.com.

85 With permission from Janet Thompson. Janet Thompson is a speaker and author of eighteen books, including the Woman to Woman Mentoring resources.

86 With permission from Janet Thompson.

87 Rick Warren, *The Purpose Driven Life, What On Earth Am I Here For?* (Grand Rapids, Michigan: Zondervan, 2002), 19.

88 Ibid., 83.

Chapter 13

89 https://www.blueletterbible.org/lang/lexicon/lexicon.cfm?Strongs=G1515&t=KJV.

90 John Ortberg, *The Me I Want To Be, Becoming God's Best Version of You* (Grand Rapids, Michigan: Zondervan, 2010), 117.

91 Michael Van Dyke, *The Story of Dietrich Bonhoeffer* (Uhrichsville, Ohio: Barbour Publishing, Inc., 2001), 188.

92 http://www.brainyquote.com/quotes/authors/m/mother_teresa.html, October 5, 2015.

Epilogue

93 Heidi McLaughlin, *Sand to Pearls, Making Bold Choices to Enrich Your Life* (Sisters, Oregon: Deep River Books, 2010), 230, 231.

CPSIA information can be obtained
at www.ICGtesting.com
Printed in the USA
FSOW01n1925150616
21617FS